Socialists have more power when the game is played with votes than when it is played with dollars. The fundamental thrust of any socialist economic strategy should be to switch the terrain of debate toward the game that is played with votes.

The Alligator Strategy

Alligators lie in a watering hole with just their eyes sticking out. The water buffaloes come down to drink. The water buffalo puts its foot in the water. The alligator grabs the foot. A tremendous struggle ensues. The water buffalo is defenceless if pulled into the water. The alligator, if pulled up onto the land, will get stomped.

That's the game we're playing. We have to pull capital into the water. We have to understand that there are some terrains on which we are much stronger than others.

– Samuel Bowles

DEMOCRATIC SOCIALISM

DEMOCRATIC SOCIALISM
The Challenge of the Eighties and Beyond

Proceedings of a Conference
Sponsored by the Boag Foundation

EDITED BY DONNA WILSON

NEW STAR BOOKS
VANCOUVER, CANADA

 2

First Printing August 1985
1 2 3 4 5 89 88 87 86 85

Canadian Cataloguing in Publication Data
Main entry under title:
Democratic socialism, the challenge of the
eighties and beyond

Conference held October 1983, in Vancouver, B.C.
Includes index.
ISBN 0-919573-44-4 (bound).
–ISBN 0-919573-45-2 (pbk.)
1. Socialism – Congresses. I. Wilson, Donna, 1944-
II. Boag Foundation.
HX13.D45 1983 320.5'315 C85-091296-2

New Star titles are published
with assistance from the Canada Council.

Printed and bound in Canada
by Broadway Printers, Vancouver

New Star Books Ltd.
2504 York Avenue
Vancouver, B.C.
Canada V6K 1E3

Allan Boag arrived in Vancouver from Scotland in 1894, and worked at his trade as a foundryman until the recession in 1918. He spent several years as a self-employed grocer and nurseryman, acquiring properties throughout Vancouver. The subsequent increase in value of these properties made Boag a man of modest wealth. Allan Boag died at age 85, in 1944. True to the views he had formed about the failings of the prevailing economic and social system, Boag turned over all of his possessions to a trust.

The objectives of the Boag Foundation, the furtherance of workers' education in the fields of history, economics, social and political economy and trade union organization, reflect Allan Boag's belief that an enlightened people wedded to the democratic process could achieve a humane and equitable society.

In publishing Democratic Socialism: The Challenge of the Eighties and Beyond, *the Directors believe that another significant step is being taken toward making the vision of Allan Boag a reality.*

HAROLD WINCH   DAVID STUPICH   JIM MCKENZIE

CONTENTS

PREFACE

Donna Wilson
Editor

THE CONFERENCE "DEMOCRATIC SOCIALISM – The Challenge of the Eighties and Beyond," held in Vancouver, October 20-23, 1983, was sponsored and organized by the Boag Foundation and gave rise to this book. Jim McKenzie, a Director of the Foundation, coordinated the project from its original conception through to the publication of this book. His guidance was truly democratic and his patience seemingly inexhaustible. Yvonne Cocke undertook the administrative organization with her usual, but nonetheless remarkable, equanimity and efficiency. Maurice Gibbons, Challenge Education Associates, Simon Fraser University, provided the conceptual basis for an egalitarian conference designed to produce a book.

A variety of resource support was provided through the contributions of 162 invited and self-selected participants who were asked to determine, discuss and record their views on the issues confronting democratic socialists. All resource people shared their expertise in formal and informal discussions. Some prepared formal papers which were duplicated and distributed to all conference participants. Of those who wrote papers, many made oral presentations to plenary or discussion groups. Some presentations differed substantially from the papers, others did not. An editor's note indicates whether a formal paper has been revised for the purpose of this volume. Where the presentation differed substantially or completely from the paper, that too has been noted. Some presentations were made by individuals who had not submitted papers. Only those participants who were invited to make presentations to plenary or discussion groups have been identified in the text. (Unedited transcripts of all papers are available to interested readers. An order form can be found at the back of the book.)

Participants divided into four self-selected groups. Each group undertook to focus on one of four broad categories: the People, the Economy, the Government and the World. Through a loosely enforced agenda, each group was requested to determine the most significant issues facing democratic socialists in the 1980s, to discuss the substance and implications of these issues and to generate tentative policy recommendations. The structure of the book was determined by the structure of the conference. The four parts correspond to the broad discussion categories. The chapters contain material derived from audio tapes, discussion papers, and written notes and summary statements from each of the discussion groups.

The dynamics of oral deliberation among people of diverse opinions and backgrounds cannot easily be appropriated by traditional prose continuity. The primary editorial consideration has been to capture the spirit and content of the conference through translation from the spoken to the written word. No attempt has been made to homogenize opinions or conclusions, to eliminate contradictions, or to imply solutions where none was reached. For many participants the conference was an arduous and provocative exercise. We hope the book is merely provocative.

D.W.
April 17, 1985

PROLOGUE

Jim McKenzie
Director
The Boag Foundation

IN ISSUING THE CALL FOR THE CONFERENCE, out of which this book developed, the Directors of the Boag Trust saw a need, not only to examine our roots, but to press forward into the future and explore the world crisis and to develop a socialist response of a Canadian character.

1983 was a year of nostalgia. Centenary conferences revealed the many faces of Marx. In 1883, the year that Marx died and John Maynard Keynes was born, the Fabian Society was founded in London and William Morris helped establish the Social Democratic Federation. Henry George had published *Progress and Poverty,* which persuasively laid out the famous "single tax" or tax on land theory. These men and organizations profoundly shaped the thoughts of succeeding generations.

The CCF/NDP 50th Anniversary Convention in Regina paid tribute to its founders and their educating zeal. Fifty years ago Calvin Coolidge died and was replaced by Franklin D. Roosevelt;

Adolph Hitler became the Chancellor of Germany; the cast of players was being assembled for World War II. In Germany the ring of steel snapped shut. Trade unions and other political parties were suppressed; books were burnt; the barbed wire compounds of concentration camps were erected. In such an industrious and civilized culture, one which had introduced sickness insurance under Bismarck in 1883, 92 percent of the German electorate voted for the Nazis.

In literature, George Bernard Shaw produced *On the Rocks* and H.G. Wells projected *The Shape of Things to Come*. George Orwell's *Down and Out in Paris and London* contrasted with the dream-like utopia of Shangri-la in James Hilton's *Lost Horizon*.

At the same time, Franklin D. Roosevelt produced *Looking Forward* as a practical answer for a generation reared on Edward Bellamy's 1887 utopia, *Looking Backward,* which, of course, was the tale of an apolitical Rip Van Winkle who awoke to find technology had solved all the problems of production and distribution. No one believes that any more. One hears that the answer lies in the human breast, but few believe it. Democracy is not fully trusted within our political and economic institutions, especially when superior organization can be used as a substitute till the real thing comes along. This very skimpy review of the century and the half-century is designed to show you something you already know—how difficult it is to change patterns of behaviour of both rulers and the ruled.

A look at the slightly shorter span of 40 years, the life of the Boag Trust, presents us with the same conflicts. By 1943, the "phony war" had developed into a full-scale conflagration. Sisyphus-like, Harold Laski was writing *Reflections on the Revolution of our Time*. Keynes unveiled his plan for an international currency. There was the zoot suit with the "reet pleat" and the world sang "Mairzy Doats" and "Comin' in on a Wing and a Prayer."

Wages, prices and salaries were frozen in the United States to forestall inflation. The same government ordered mines to be taken over when half a million miners downed tools. Even within the increased scope of acceptable intervention in a wartime economy, capitalism had a very limited response to social problems.

In invoking these various images of the past, you would swear that we had come full circle on the great mandala. Once again the conservative right is claiming the public's attention. The marketplace falters under a mountain of international debt. Bewildered and politically ignorant populations seek solace in outmoded political and economic theories or find succour in the bosom of a church. We witness the first phase before the anger sets in. What then? Anarchy! Are we equipped to catch the rising tide of the protest?

When I was young, we socialists had *all* the answers. My induction into the Co-operative Commonwealth Federation 30 years ago was attended by interminable discussions about means and ends, about the moral requirements of socialism, about the corrosive effects of power, the power of money, the power of office, the power of the state. We contrived to have checks and balances built into our organizations. In the building of the "New Jerusalem" we demanded that "our people" behave like Caesar's wife, beyond reproach. Were we so naive to believe that we could design institutions that were, if not stainless, at least stain resistant? Our opponents sneered at our "holier than thou" attitude, but we took it as a compliment and went about our business of eliminating the privilege of elites. A society without classes is what we saw. After all, our vision explained history and economics; it put power and people as a jewel in its democratic setting.

Each and all of us were able to give a reasonable explanation of how the capitalist system, with its primitive technology of money, exploited working people. We formed part of a great world movement that promised to revolutionize the way of doing business and to alter the contractual relationship of society.

I was very happy with that state of affairs and would like us to recapture something of that complete view of humanity which has been fractured by our political accommodations and our loss of purity of purpose. That does not demand a saintly idealism, but a reappraisal of the great shift in scientific discovery, "The Cosmic Code," that brought forth our marvelous new technology and its social consequences. If we are to combat the cynicism that is abroad, we have to be more than poll readers and slick technicians. While these skills are important, they are not nearly as sustaining as understanding what we are about and translating our knowledge into a socialist credo that can save our civilization. We have to become teachers once again.

We are not prepared to allow a repeat of the lost years of the Great Depression, but will start to broadcast a coherent plan to extend human freedom. We will halt the return to breadlines and food banks and moves to throw the dispossessed to charity. We will not stand idle while social wealth is siphoned off to produce weapons which will destroy our planet. The world was almost reduced to a whimper when people were swept up in the madness of Nazi Germany, a "democratic" nation mesmerized by "a man on horseback." A strong leader with an immaculate organization used all the trappings of the state to glorify superiority and to silence all opposition. We came very close to entering a new dark age. We came within a historical whisker of witnessing the exchange of atomic weapons. The people of Hiroshima and Nagasaki felt the blast waves of the New World. The rest of humanity escaped only to face the next generation of nuclear weapons. The struggles for socialism and for peace have never been more inextricable. We have to see to it that we go out with neither a whimper nor a bang.

The snarling dogs of war are on a taut leash held by infirm men who may lose touch with reality. Willy Brandt, President of the Socialist International, says it very eloquently in *The Search For Peace:*

> The safeguarding of peace forms the basic condition for everything else to which we aspire; without peace everything else becomes an illusion!

Without peace all else comes to nought. The great wars shattered international solidarity between workers and rebuilding was hampered by the antics of nations. The events of yesterday impart some urgency to our ongoing search. The people who came before us were better equipped to deal with radical changes–only the revolution never came.

J.M.
March 29, 1985

DEMOCRATIC SOCIALISM
The Challenge of the Eighties and Beyond

I
THE PEOPLE

TECHNOLOGY
Alternatives Within Our Capability*

George McRobie
Intermediate Technology Development Group
London, U.K.

IT IS IMPORTANT TO REMEMBER the traditions of socialism and to emphasize particularly that the preoccupation with purely economic mechanisms is a relatively recent phenomenon and one which I think leads us along the wrong track. We need to broaden the concept of socialism to include things other than simply large-scale public ownership of economic activity and discussions about economic efficiency. We must once again begin to think in original concepts of socialism– the ideals of liberty, equality and fraternity.

We need to enlarge the concept of what we mean by socialism today because we have been forced to defend our position in terms of premises dictated by the people who

* The article "Technology: Alternatives Within Our Capability" is an edited transcription of George McRobie's speech to the opening plenary session of the conference. Mr. McRobie also prepared an excellent paper for the conference–"Technology for Rich Countries"–which is available from the Boag Foundation.

own capital. Questions of social justice have steadily given way to discussions about equality of opportunity. We should not be talking about opportunity, we should be talking about equality.

My area of expertise allows me to relate the premises of socialism to technology, particularly as it relates to Third World countries. I work with the Intermediate Technology Development Group, which was formed in the mid-1960s in London. At that time the common theory, if you can call it a theory, about the development of poor countries was the "trickle down effect." You adopt the technology of the west and somehow the riches that this creates will trickle down to the people downstairs. Hans Singer, of the University of Sussex, tried to establish ground rules for development economists: no one would develop a plan for a country unless he had at least flown over it once by daylight. Even that was a problem.

The technologies of the west, sold or given to poor countries, were in many cases damaging or destroying rural and cultural structures. Aid and development was bypassing the great majority of the rural poor and concentrating development in the cities. Today, organizations like the World Bank, who still have a sneaking love for the growth of cities, tell us that, based on present trends, Mexico City will have a population of 30 million people by the year 2000. Many other cities will be above fifteen million. That is, in fact, an impossibility. Long before cities reach that size the infrastructure collapses. The water supply, the sewage, the roads, disintegrate and the air becomes unbreathable. Above all, a city of 30 million people presupposes that there are 30 million people outside the city producing twice as much food as they need. There aren't and there will not be 30 million people in Mexico producing excess food, particularly under the hammer blows of the International Monetary Fund [IMF] and international money lenders who are desperately trying to squeeze out some sort of interest on their loans.

It is apparent that the western industrial technologies simply don't work for poor countries. Analysis done by groups such as the Prague Commission, Global 2000 and World

Employment Reports strongly suggests that the developing world is heading for disaster under current aid and development programs.

Financial indebtedness has distorted the economies of developing countries and our own economies. Instead of concentrating on the needs of the poor for food, shelter, clothing and basic community services, aid and development have exported technologies which are beginning to compete with western countries. False protectionism on the part of the rich ensures that the results of development accrue to a very small number of people in the poor countries. It would be correct to say that overseas aid consists of taking money from poor people in rich countries and giving it to rich people in poor countries. We need to think very seriously about what we are doing to the developing world and what we are doing to ourselves in the process. It's a reasonable bet that the international money lenders are preparing national governments, that is, taxpayers, to bail out of bad debts. A large number of countries must default on their debts; they have no option. Pumping money into a banking system that has lost a lot of money could release an inflationary force in our own countries the like of which we haven't seen for a long time.

We need to look at how we can support the development of poor countries so that the next generation, our children, will benefit from increased trade with them as equals. The type of overseas aid we have pursued leads to the horrendous gunboat diplomacy of the United States. Assisting developing countries by supplying the most reactionary governments with arms is generating military revolutionary movements all over the world. The alternatives are policies which actually help the rural poor to earn a living. That is not beyond our capability.

There are technologies which do address the needs of the rural poor. They are small, because they deal with small communities. They are fairly simple, because they are to be owned, operated and managed by people who are not highly sophisticated, in our sense of the word at least. They are capital-saving, because the rural poor have plenty of labour but are short of capital. Within engineering limits they are non-violent toward people and the environment. They are the exact opposite of technologies developed in the west over the past one hundred years. Western technologies are big and growing bigger, they are capital and energy intensive and becoming more so, and they are singularly violent toward people and the environment. They exclude more and more people from effective ownership and control.

The concept of capital-saving is a totally new one. Our industrial structure has been built on cheap, highly mobile energy, in the form of oil. One of our most urgent tasks is to help developing countries not to get hooked on that kind of energy because in a hundred years it's not going to be there, and in ten years they won't be able to afford it. If we hooked developing countries on energy-intensive agriculture, all world oil reserves would virtually disappear within the next 50-60 years.

Perhaps we also need to start looking at different forms of technology. Canada was one of the first countries to take an interest in appropriate technologies. In 1968, a conference on the application of small scale technology in industrialized countries was held in St. John's, Newfoundland. Scientists who had previously supported the concept of limitless growth based on an infinite supply of oil began to acknowledge that the environment cannot stand a widespread replication of western technology based on fossil fuels. There is, of course, enough coal in the world for us to be able to do without oil, although its uneven distribution over the face of the earth is a problem. A much bigger problem is that the use of coal would result in industrial pollution the likes of which would make the present problem look like a picnic. We have the technology to strip the world of its forests and to remove the topsoil from the land. Violent technology has not only begun to strip the world of non-renewable resources, but is making many renewable resources potentially non-renewable.

Technology can solve many of these problems. After we have admitted that acid rain exists, we can introduce technology that will eliminate it. However, our electricity and steel will become very much more expensive than they are now. We need to pay close attention to the problem of internalizing the environmental costs of our industry. There is marked reluctance by the labour movement to take up issues of environmental pollution, because the owners of industry say, "jobs or environment–take your pick." We are frightened and take industry's word that there is a conflict between jobs and environmental control. In fact, the employment-creating potential in a thoroughgoing program of energy conservation is very much larger than the employment-creating potential of large-scale projects in the field of energy. We must press environmental questions in political discussions, particularly in discussions with the owners of large-scale industry. The environmental movement has been effective. Fifteen years ago you couldn't have a discussion about the environment. Today it is, at least to some extent, built into our thinking.

We must reintroduce questions about the character of work. We need to start looking at human ecology as it relates to the nature and organization of work. What are organizations that enable people to work well together like? Generally speaking they are not large. We need to experiment with forms of ownership. We need to look at where work is done. Future generations will regard the concentration of productive activity in cities as one of our more outstanding aberrations. Urban concentration is made possible by cheap oil, which allows us to regard the cost of transport as negligible. As oil reserves decline, the cost of transport will escalate.

I've noticed with delight that at least a hundred small breweries have been started in Britain over the past five or six years, just when the big brewers had built enormous breweries to serve the whole country. Since beer consists rather more than 90 percent of water, they have suddenly discovered that with petrol costing two pounds per gallon, carting water all over the country is a rather expensive caper. I'm sure they are now working on dehydrated beer, but in the meantime lots of small breweries have started serving their own specific areas. Economic forces are working in favour of the small and localized and against the highly centralized.

The costs of concentrating population in cities are prodigious. Chicago is a bit worried about the state of its drains. Chicago was built, during a period of cheap and abundant labour, on a marsh and is supported by vast numbers of brick arches under which the sewage system runs. The system is beginning to collapse. Current replacement costs would be at least comparable to the construction of the Alaska pipeline. One city can't afford that. Is it not possible to think in terms of a more rational distribution of people over the country?

We need first to determine the circumstances under which people can be shown to work more productively and more creatively. Secondly, we need to look at the geographical location of work and, thirdly, at the social organization of work. A small piece of enabling legislation in Britain, which was snuck through just before the demise of the last Labour government, has resulted in about 500 small industrial co-operatives which have had an incredible survival rate. Private small companies have a very low survival rate. Small co-operatives have a very strong survival line because their prime objective is not the private appropriation of wealth. Their prime objective is to produce socially useful products or services and to provide interesting and agreeable employment. The Highland Development Fund, which was started with money left by an American bootlegger, is specifically directed to assisting carpenters and fishermen buy and renew equipment. Its purpose is to maintain life in the rural areas of the West Highlands. In the United States, Local Initiatives Support was started with a $6 million grant from the Ford Foundation. Its purpose is not to accumulate wealth but to support socially desirable local activities where the return is not measured solely in terms of money. Part of the return may be to create jobs for young people and to stimulate local activity. The return on capital may be only 6 or 8 percent, but the economic return, as distinct from the commercial return, is very substantial indeed. We must not be hoodwinked by people who say, "This isn't viable; it's not making 20 percent." That is hokum of the highest order.

How do we mobilize local resources to give people greater control over their local economic environment? What forms of ownership are appropriate? There are probably as many forms of ownership as there are industries. As well as the traditional socialist concepts of co-operatives and worker owners, there is no reason why we shouldn't have municipal and community ownership.

Ownership patterns need no longer be dictated by technology. The technologist can produce almost anything you want him to produce, to any scale. In India, I recently attended the opening of the world's first mini-cement plant which produces twenty tons (as opposed to two to three thousand tons) of first class Portland cement per day. The project took about five years to complete, in the face of stiff opposition from the World Bank, the Indian Government, most of the international agencies and the cement industry. We have done the same with sugar refining. You can do the same with glass production. It is possible to take large scale industries and scale them down.

I am not saying that everything big is bad. We must sort out what must be big and what can be small. People don't, on the whole, enjoy working in big organizations, particularly if the technology is monstrous and inhumane, as it is, say, in the car industry. When I worked in the coal mines, we used to organize worker education groups to visit other industries. One of the visits we made was to the Ford works. Miners, working three and four thousand feet under ground in very dangerous conditions in the 1940s, came back absolutely appalled by the conditions under which these people worked. None of them would have given up his job to work in a car factory, where people spent ten-hour shifts on an assembly line drilling the same three holes interminably. Technology is perfectly capable of making cars which last twenty years. We could shift a very large part of the labour force to automotive maintenance, which is a local and small-scale activity.

We need to encourage the development of technology assessment teams to determine the impact of technology, not simply on profits, but on people, the environment and resources. We must ask if a technology leads to democratic or authoritarian forms of ownership. If you subjected certain technologies, such as nuclear energy, to questions of this kind, they wouldn't come out very well. Nuclear energy is possible only in a highly authoritarian industrial environment.

I have lived just long enough to be able to see in many European countries and in certain parts of North America renewed shades of the Weimar Republic. There is evidence that we are again moving into a very authoritarian society with highly centralized industry, ownership and government, with very large unions which are really the creatures of big industry. If we don't look at the nature of work, where it's done and how it's done, and the technology which is being pushed onto us in the name of inevitability, we are headed toward a more and more authoritarian society. We have to move rapidly to find practical, not theoretical, effective ways of decentralizing economic power.

THE FUTURE OF THE WELFARE STATE*

Joop den Uyl
Former Prime Minister
The Netherlands

THE WELFARE STATE IS UNDER HEAVY FIRE. It is important to realize that the assault began before the current period of stagnation in the world economy. It would be incorrect to ascribe criticism of the welfare state solely to problems connected with the present world economic crisis. However, economic and social policy issues are not unrelated. The welfare state will not survive if we do not find jobs for everybody who wants to work. Full employment will be achieved only if the ramifications of technological change are addressed through a drastic shortening of working hours. In many ways it is true that the growth of the welfare state was a byproduct of the economic expansion experienced after the Second World War, and that we will have to restore some growth to safeguard it. Industrialized countries must organize limited

* Mr. den Uyl's paper "The Future of the Welfare State" was read to a plenary session of the conference. It is presented here with some minor revisions.

but sustained growth of the international economy and world trade, giving major priority to the growth of the economies of developing countries.

It was apparent in 1970 that the social order, as it had developed after the Second World War, was meeting opposition across a wide front. The paternalistic nature of government intervention, the rapid growth of the public sector at the expense of the market sector and the philosophy of equality and justice were seen as impinging on a "natural" social order in which the inequality of individuals and the ability of people to look after themselves were the norm.

This countermovement was manifest in both the economy and in economic policy as well as in criticism of welfare facilities in the field of health care, education, social services and socio-cultural activities. In the economy, the counter-movement is associated with monetarism and a reduction in government spending. In the social field, stress is laid on privatization, the recovery of private initiative and emphasis on the value of voluntary work. On the ideological front, social democracy, which is seen as the defender and the embodiment of the welfare state, has been under attack. When sociologists and political scientists point to the welfare state as the cause of all the ills of modern society, from unemployment and growing criminality to the deterioration in human relations, they are also pointing the finger at socialists.

What do we actually mean by the social welfare state? Let us begin with a definition of the welfare state as a constitutional system operating on four principles:

1. **Social Security:** protection of the individual against the risks of the modern industrial society such as unemployment, illness and disability.
2. **Social Provision:** basic facilities necessary to every individual, such as food, housing, education and health care.
3. **Welfare:** promotion of individual well-being to enable people to pursue their own aspirations and take part in politics, culture, sport.

4. **Equality:** promotion of a righteous distribution of income.

In the 50s and 60s, political action and economic growth made it possible to increase justice and more equal opportunities for all. Provisions and insurances were created to guarantee at least minimal security in the event of illness, disability or unemployment, and for the elderly. Education, health care, social work and cultural amenities were expanded. With the expansion came a rise in the share of the national income spent or redistributed by government.

Economic intervention has generally increased in all the industrial countries since the Second World War. The pivotal question is not the share of national income over which governments exercise an influence. What is more important is the degree to which, and the way in which, governments managed to steer the free market. In some countries, industries were nationalized, in others there was mandatory or indicative economic planning. In almost every country, governments promoted innovative research and investment. Growing intervention in economic life was often independent of the political character of governments. Conservative governments in France undertook far-reaching indicative planning.

These activities resulted in a growing public sector and an increase in the percentage of the national income taken up by government expenditures and compulsory social insurance. The lowest increase was in the United States, the highest in Sweden. Criticism of the welfare state often focuses on what is regarded as the excessive size of the public sector. Socialism is associated with a large public sector, but it should be pointed out that public sector growth has also occurred in countries without socialist governments.

Social democrats do not hold a monopoly on the principle of government taking the lead. Although in the Netherlands, for example, extensive planning was largely inspired by the Dutch Labour Party, the contribution of the Christian Democratic Parties has been far from negligible. Indeed, the growing power of these confessional movements and the gradual rise and shaping of the welfare state coincide completely. In Britian, the development of what Beveridge termed "the social service state" cannot be understood without recognizing the co-operation between the government and private charitable initiatives, inspired by socio-liberal sentiments which gained ground in the nineteenth century as a response to the reform of the Poor Law.

Any discussion of modern parliamentary and democratic systems within which the welfare state developed cannot ignore the work of French and Anglo-Saxon thinkers who were opposed to the autocratic political systems of the seventeenth and eighteenth centuries. Their opposition was based on the conviction that individuals must be equal as citizens and that consequently no one automatically has the right to exercise power over them. Political power relations underwent major changes with the emancipation of "the proletariat" which began toward the end of the nineteenth century. Universal suffrage and the political demand for "assistance from the government" are contiguous. A Dutch author describes the welfare state as "that phase of parliamentary or presidential democracy in which the great mass of citizens, as a result of universal suffrage, demand that the government intervene to give them their fair share of the advantages that in the nineteenth century had been enjoyed by a relatively small group of citizens who at that time held all power."

Criticism of the welfare system warrants close attention. Opponents contend that swelling government bureaucracies cause the market sector's share to shrink and with it the ability to pay for the welfare structure. The tendency toward regulating more and more aspects of social as well as economic life is reflected in continuously increasing production of collective goods and services and growing control by government over the management and disbursement of the national income. In the philosophical or ideological domain, critics of the welfare state discount the ability of the state to regulate social life and point to state paternalism and lack of democratic control over the expanding welfare establishment.

Again, a historical perspective is valuable. In 1880, Wagner, in his "Gesetz der Wachsende Ausdehnung der Staatsstatigkeiten," predicted that government intervention in society would increase with progressive social and economic development. He suggested that industrialization and urbanization, concomitant with social communication becoming more dense and social relations more complex, would require more legal protection, more and better housing and a larger administration.

A more complete understanding of the current antagonism toward the welfare state may be revealed by examining perceptual ideologies. There is an increasing discrepancy between expectations and fulfillment inherent in the growing role of the state and government. Socialists in particular should be aware that the world economic crisis of the 1970s meant the end of the era of rising expectations. After 1973, when economic growth slowed to a snail's pace and rising unemployment brought about an even further sequestration of the national income by government, the problems of a big public sector became more visible. The reduction in economic growth contributed to the welfare system's inability to keep many promises made to the people. Its political credibility has been seriously undermined. As the citizenry experiences declining control over its own money, rising unemployment, increasing regulation and state paternalism, belief in the actual ability of the state to regulate social life decreases.

Socialist governments have been confronted by resistance from trade unionists and leftist interest groups. The defeat and deterioration of the British Labour Party during the second half of the 1970s cannot be seen apart from its failure to formulate and implement an Incomes Policy to protect the essentials of the welfare state. As a result of the growing discrepancy between the apparent and actual power of the bureaucracy, the number of interest groups that are taking matters into their own hands has grown rapidly. The gap between the entitlements to rights and their realization, as well as the inconsistencies between various rights, constitutes a danger for the preservation of the welfare society.

The world economic crisis of the 70s should have taught socialists that it is not possible to raise the standard of living of workers or to expand social security or fight unemployment on an isolated national basis. The essential condition of the survival of the welfare state is to overcome the present disorder of the international economy. The operation of transnational corporations has transformed the structure of the world economy. Oligopolistic corporate forces play a determinate role in the marketing and price setting of a wide variety of commodities and, according to UNCTAD sources, control 55 percent of total world trade. Transnational corporations thus limit the scope for national policy making to a very considerable extent.

Socialist parties must also address the legitimacy of the argument which suggests that social services offered under the pretext of providing for the needs of recipients actually turn them into passive, dependent welfare cases. What is needed is a "grand design" for the future: a plan of what is desirable and feasible. Future studies must concentrate on the social and cultural factors which accompany economic growth and technological development. Increased labour productivity, resulting from rapid technological development, has manifested itself in Europe, not only in a rapid infusion of jobs in service sectors, but also in a standardization of products and production methods, in environental degradation, depletion of the earth's stock of non-renewable resources and in an uprooting of traditional values in society. Our traditional faith in inevitable and desirable progress needs to be re-examined. It has been said that "further growth leads to decay of the person and the environment, to rottenness of the social fabric and the alienation of man, once satiation is reached."

Socialism has always been a movement to improve the quality of existence, not a movement for the production of ever more goods and services. The scepticism and pessimism that surround the predictions for the future of the welfare state should be an important stimulus for a reorientation in patterns of needs and scarcities.

It is time to take stock. The inventory of criticism against the welfare state bears repeating: the state has enormous powers; the public sector is crowding out the market sector; provisions can no longer be paid for; bureaucracy dominates so that democratic checks on welfare provisions are inadequate. There are choices to be made. Such criticisms can be answered by empowering governments to reduce the certainty and security which the welfare state has created. This is what we see happening at the moment in Europe and America. However, the essential features of the welfare state can be preserved through a consistent effort to decentralize welfare provisions. Reform which aims at preserving justice must engineer a balance between the public and the market sector. A return to the domination of private, economic and financial interests in the social order must be rejected.

A reformed welfare state must confine the costs of social security by consistently adhering to a policy of full employment. Unemployment jeopardizes our ability to pay for the welfare state. There must be scope for volunteers to work alongside professionals and for clients to influence the kind of provisions created in their interests. Bureaucracies are the products of large organizations. Decentralized community organizations must be self-regulating; information services should replace supervisory services. There is no reason for allowing the solidarity of a community to get bogged down in bureaucracy.

The choice for reform or dismantling of the welfare state is intimately tied up with the image one has of society in the future. If hope is solely vested in the recovery of the market economy, the corollary is neglect of the system of social provisons. To what kind of society will that lead? It will be an economy driven by the new technology with flourishing transnational business and new kinds of commercial services. It will be an economy with a high-earning elite in industry, a pervasive deterioration in existing work and mass employment. The tendency of the labour market to become segmented will not be checked. Ethnic groups, women, young people, will be allocated dirty, unpleasant work, the unskilled or semi-skilled relegated to second place, preferably to be available on demand. That is the future offered by the opponents of the welfare state. It is a vision socialists must reject.

It is still possible to imagine and achieve a society whose mark is a just distribution of work and income, a society in which everybody's right to work is respected. In this respect the revolutionary significance of the redistribution of work is misunderstood.

The reduction of the average working week to 32 hours in 1990, and perhaps to 25 hours in the year 2000, will be a gigantic operation involving radical social and cultural changes, much more so than the desperately-needed innovation in industry, the drastic reduction in energy consumption and safeguards to the environment. It will result in a completely different organization of work in industry and in the community. Numerous shift systems, longer opening hours for offices, services, factories, shops and far-reaching individualization will result in a fairer distribution of work and income at home and in the community.

This visionary society of shorter working hours and more leisure time will mean different rules, but don't imagine that the welfare state can be written off. The welfare state is not the invention of carping or wasteful government; it is the way we have chosen to express our joint responsibility to community. Joint social responsibility must continue to guarantee a living for all those who, through no fault of their own, are unable to provide for themselves but who nevertheless must not be allowed to suffer by comparison with those who have been lucky enough to escape the same fate. It is our responsibility to see that all citizens have the necessary educational opportunities which will equip them to take part in our society. The welfare state does not concern just a financial entity. The crux of the welfare state is the way in which we wish to conduct our lives together and carry joint responsibility.

Some public sector spending will have to be cut. The current manifestations and expressions of the welfare state are not sacred or inviolable. Certain aspects of the welfare state have created dependencies and are in danger of becoming paternalistic. The social security systems in some countries are on the brink of collapse because they are founded on social assumptions that are no longer realistic. The welfare state must adjust to developments such as individualization, an increasing older population, redefined family units and the growing instability in relationships. There are many reasons for re-evaluating and reassessing the welfare state, but the re-evaluation must be done so that the essential features and objectives of the welfare state are preserved and, where necessary, restored.

The essential features of the modern welfare state should be the guarantee of a living, a just allocation of burdens, and increased influence over administrative and policy concerns for the recipients of social services. Additionally, the most vulnerable groups in society must have free access to basic social institutions. This is exactly what is *not* happening under right wing governments at present. In Holland, for example, library services are being drastically reduced, family help and child care are becoming luxury items, and access to basic educational facilities is seriously at risk. School fees are being introduced for a provision which is regarded as so socially essential that it is compulsory.

The repercussions of cuts in welfare services hit hardest, and with cynical regularity, at those for whom the welfare state was primarily intended. We are seeing the beginnings of a fundamentally different ordering of our society in which common responsibility and care for the weak will no longer be given priority, but where survival of the fittest is regarded as the norm and in which self-interest and self-assertiveness are the paramount virtues. It is a bitter and historic move in the growth and development of our society.

In the western world social democracy has been blamed for the crisis. This is political deceit and blackmail. The crisis has occurred in public sectors varying drastically in size and where government responsibilities have been extremely diverse in their scope. It would seem that as the memory of the Second World War fades, a generation is emerging which is reverting to social conditions characteristic of the heyday of capitalism. When economic progress is at stake, some are prepared to pay the price of inequality, discrimination, the polarization of opposing attitudes and the escalation of social conflict.

Social democracy must look ahead and understand that with progressive technological developments the right to work and income, to a secure living and to health care can be maintained only if responsibilities are demarcated clearly. Society and the state has a responsibility for ensuring a secure living and full employment. In return, the people have a duty to society beyond their claim on government and the state. Social democracy must crystallize and promulgate the basis on which choices are to be made, and need not be ashamed of the welfare state which it has helped bring about. It must reform the welfare state and preserve it against the ideology of egoism, which is aimed at its downfall. Restructuring world order and defending a common responsibility for society as a whole is the way to safeguard the future of the welfare state.

MORAL CONSERVATISM*

Evan Simpson
Philosophy Department
McMaster University
Hamilton, Ontario
Vice President
New Democratic Party
Ontario

THE STRUCTURE OF THIS CONFERENCE is a model that social democrats should take very seriously in coming years. We must
develop better institutions for public discussions. My
approach is philosophical and my discussion extends far
beyond the 1980s, but despite its broad scope and philosophical nature, it is quite practical. The gap between
intellectually valid solutions to social problems and public
acceptance of the solutions makes it very difficult to implement social democratic ideas and programs. We spend a lot of

* The article "Moral Conservatism" is an edited transcription of Prof.
Simpson's presentation to the discussion group which focused on The
People. In his paper "Prospects for a Moral Economy", Prof. Simpson
elaborates on many of the ideas presented here. The paper is available from
the Boag Foundation.

time developing policies and programs, but we don't really try hard enough to understand the gap between our certainty and pervasive public doubt about our approach.

The case against laissez-faire, free market governments and economies, has been made many times. The effects of an unregulated economy are too devastating to be tolerated. Human well-being depends upon a measure of social rationality and public planning for objectives that we collectively agree upon. The essence of the argument against collective public action is that it is impossible because our society is too diverse. In a pluralistic society there is structural lack of agreement about social objectives. We can discuss this objection seriously only if we understand how deeply conservative human beings are.

The kinds of economic radicalism and social programs socialists advocate are possible only if we take social conservatism seriously. The conservative instinct is rooted in the feelings and emotions that define human beings and give events meaning. When we fear events, we see them as threatening and seek security from danger. When we pity other persons, we see their distress as unacceptable and want to relieve it. When we experience curiosity, we see things as novel and want to know more. There is very little that we want which can't be traced to these emotionally determined purposes. There are no basic social institutions that are not expressions of these purposes.

The institution of property exists largely because ownership provides security for people. Institutions of care and provision are natural outgrowths of compassionate desires. Educational institutions developed, not only because they promote the continuity of socially necessary techniques, but also because they respond to the thirst for knowledge. Political conservatives and socialists do not necessarily disagree about the importance of these institutions. Where we disagree is the form these institutions should take. Should institutions of relief be private charity or ought they to be publicly organized around a broadly based system of welfare?

Social institutions make our fundamental purposes coherent and valid. Our feelings aren't always in order. We mistakenly fear things. We pity people who don't need that attention. We can test the validity of our feelings by reference to certain expectations. Societal norms enable us to see when a person is suffering unduly and therefore warrants compassion and relief. Without behavioural norms, and without the stable expectations they make reasonable, we could not justify our beliefs or our purposes.

The conservative connection provides the stability that makes judgments about our purposes possible. Established social practices and institutions provide good reasons to want to avoid rapid or uncontrolled change in patterns of life and expectations generally. Only when there is a certain social stability can we live with confidence and purpose. Unfortunately, we can't control change very well. Socialists always ask themselves if it is possible to control and regulate social development in a way that corresponds to these conservative instincts. The answer is yes, it is possible, at least in principle, because there is agreement about purposes, at least in the abstract. Contrary to the suggestion that in a pluralistic society there is no consensus on purposes, we do at least agree that people need security and education.

However, we lack practical agreement about these purposes. People in different social and economic circumstances interpret these needs quite differently. Marx said that our needs had a historical and a moral aspect. We interpret that according to our different circumstances. We cannot generate practical agreement simply by devising economic strategies which, if implemented, would generate common expectations. These political strategies do not connect with the realities of everyday life and the divergent understandings that various social groups have of security. This is a basic barrier to egalitarian mass movements. We do not understand concepts like security in the same way and therefore cannot agree on the social policies that would take us toward a guarantee of these needs.

The socialist project has as its central component the analysis of social structures which provides a context for description of a good society and a galaxy of programs meant to advance such a society. This vast intellectual and political effort avails us little unless we can solve a central paradox. All versions of our analysis identify a lopsided structure of wealth and power which impairs our capacity to take part in mutually meaningful activities. The economic structure hampers the consensus that is necessary for adequate planning. Therefore an essential condition for progress is permanently unsatisfied. It is all very well to describe the programs which a rational society would employ in order to eliminate divisive inequalities, but if these inequalities frustrate the formation of common purpose, then the best laid plans are going to prove unworkable.

For the last twenty years on this continent, socialism has largely been an academic exercise. The impulse to preserve gives us reason to expect the state to intervene in order to protect the social environment. This form of state intervention is not at all the same thing as social planning. The concept of intervention prejudices the case for planning from the very beginning. Intervention is always an exceptional act. It is an intrusion justified by the situation having gotten out of hand. A population sympathetic to charges of government interference can respond very happily to a New Deal, or wage restraints or any of a variety of programs that seem to respond to a current crisis. There is public acceptance of intervention when it is clearly necessary.

All political philosophers agree that state intervention is part of the role of government. It is an important agreement because it says that social policy and economic policy impinge upon one another. The right to property is always tied to the public interest. All political persuasions advocate a moral economy. The market is always subject to restrictions called for by recognized rights–human rights. The state is obliged to intervene to protect these rights. Unhappily the lack of consensus about social direction makes the so-called public interest very difficult to identify. It is always a matter of argument and so we see Reaganites and Thatcherites arguing that their programs are in the public interest.

The new conservative argument is one which the left is very poorly placed to win. Our difficulty can be seen in the breakdown of what used to be a consensus on equity and growth. There has been a protracted contest about the relative shares which should go to labour and to capital. It remained subdued for a number of years while continuous economic growth permitted equity to be pursued through the welfare state. With economic disruption we see these things becoming divergent options. We have to choose between equity or growth. In a system of social organization that is defined broadly by the relationship between labour and capital, the choice has to favour profits and growth. It is in the public interest to advocate increased profits and to stimulate growth. In an important sense the new right is correct because everybody depends upon the system. Even governments whose hearts are on the left have to acknowledge this fact. In France, monetarist and conservative policies are forcing the government to behave in ways very different from those they would prefer.

There is a broad consensus on the left that the state should emphasize a function which has had a legitimate, but minor, role in the past. As well as necessary intervention, the state has dabbled in production. By stressing the function of production, a government, as an economic power, gains more capacity to engage in significant social planning than if it depends upon legislation alone. The concept of direct state involvement in production informs the moral economy for social democracy and leads to its distinctive programs and approach. This approach is better called participation than intervention because it does not simply respond in emergencies. The priority of the economic system over social policy is built into the concept of intervention.

Social democratic governments envision a continual, intimate relationship with all the spheres of productive activity. The programmatics of this participation differ, of course. Canadian socialism tends to emphasize direct public investment which ought to bring socially beneficial effects to the business environment. This differs significantly from approaches taken elsewhere, for example, the Swedish experiment with wage earners funds. All such strategies of public participation aim at making corporate rationality dependent upon social rationality.

The programmatics of socialism have very significant limitations. There are limits imposed upon what a country can do by the international nature of the new economy. When corporate behaviour extends beyond national boundaries it is very difficult for an individual political jurisdiction to formulate rational economic and social policies because they can never predict what the transnational corporations are going to do. However, despite the limitations on public planning and social rationality, public participation can be patently efficient in many cases rather than inefficient as the economists of the new right would have us believe. There is plentiful national and international evidence to corroborate the strong positive correlation between public planning and economic performance.

An expanded intervention/participation argument is a technical response to technical problems. It touches only peripherally the political problems that have to be solved if our programs are ever to be implemented to any significant degree. However valid they may be, technical solutions to technical problems do not overcome public resistance to government participation and they will not until we come to terms with some significant moral and philosophical problems.

If socialist objectives are to be realized they must be founded on a premise other than economic. Moral appeals to equality are not, by themselves, any more convincing than technical economic arguments. We can search for a non-economic premise in terms of the goals that give meaning to life and in terms of the social institutions that enable us to pursue these goals. That having been said, all of the deep problems are still unanswered. Vital human purposes are subject to a variety of interpretations. People from different economic strata have different expectations. There is no general agreement on the conditions of security. Uneven distribution of income makes the understanding of the conditions of security different between the rich and poor. If one expects to be jobless from time to time, then occasional unemployment will be understood as an acceptable condition. It will be very difficult to justify social expenditures which are meant to correct patterns of deprivation to which people have become accustomed. Consequently, appeals to an industrial strategy tend to be ineffective. They occur within a context in which people have gradually become accustomed to lessened expectations and the mere suggestion that those expectations can be reversed does not touch upon what is fundamentally significant.

Common expectations and purposes are necessary if social planning is to be possible. However, the generation of these purposes is complex. Simple promises and visions of material improvement do not have a great deal of meaning or much power to motivate. Historians like E.P. Thompson have noted that working class movements have been sustained not by bread and butter issues, but by issues "in which such values as traditional customs, justice, independence, security or family autonomy were at stake". In order to translate economic distress into political action, it has to be expressed not in terms of a lower unemployment rate or higher wages, but rather in terms of standards available through popular institutions–religious sects, labour unions, ethnic communities and the like.

Social democratic parties have traditionally looked to co-operatives and trade unions as vehicles of change. They have not paid sufficient attention to institutions of discourse. We should examine the kind of discussions that go on between labour and management. Currently, in Canada, we have an adversarial system in which both sides attempt to secure the greatest gains for themselves. This does not correspond to the ideal of rational discussion which is essential for building the kinds of social consensus which are the *sine qua non* of rational planning.

In what direction should organized labour move to develop more rational discourse while still protecting their members? Participation entails government drawing free enterprise into the public well. Therefore, we are going to have to clarify our views about collective bargaining without succumbing to the myth that Canadian wage rates seriously impair our economic performance. It is obvious that industrial planning has to impinge upon the price of labour. In return, labour would presumably expect an extension of collective bargaining to cover matters presently left off the negotiating agenda. Collective bargaining would come to consider matters like the size of the work force, companies' investment decisions, and how a board of directors works. Whereas current free collective bargaining is just a compromise between competing interests, an extended form of bargaining is characteristic of rational discussion. It is a form of discussion that seeks consensus rather than compromise on the basis of such shared objectives as the viability of the firm. This second mode of discussion is characteristic of a rational society. Governments can promote this kind of rational discussion by legislatively expanding the areas which are subject to negotiation in collective agreements. By doing so, governments would be engaging in a publicly acceptable form of legislative involvement and would be helping to institutionalize a wider form of rational discussion in which mutually satisfying agreements are sought. Society would come to expect agreement rather than conflict.

DISCUSSION

NEW VOICE: How can you convince trade unions, which are in good bargaining positions and have job security, to accept an Incomes Policy in the interest of reducing inflation for the national good? In the short term, they are relatively better off as things are. How do we sell the idea that in the long run union members and their children would be better off if there were full employment and relative equality?

SIMPSON: How we can sell it is not something I can easily define. Labour has to reach that conclusion by itself and there are signs that it is moving in that direction. John Fryer discusses these issues in his paper, as does Peter Warrian, who says in his paper:

> The state, therefore, has to take over the functions
> of mobilizing and channeling capital to assure
> sufficient investment of the right kind, identified

by planning at the national, sectoral and enterprise levels, through instruments such as public enterprises. Similarly, the unions cannot confine themselves to traditional wage and working conditions issues. Nor can they agree to wage restraint without the power to assure that the released resources are used for needed investments. Unions must accordingly participate in planning at all levels, in a variety of ways including representation but primarily through collective bargaining.*

We are looking at something that extends well beyond the 80s. We are describing the development of the reorganization of the way in which we do business in this country and that is going to take a much longer time than we would like. We have to continue the argument.

NEW VOICE: You did not address the fact that we are in a capitalist political economy which is characterized by conflict. Labour/management relations are not necessarily irrational because they are adversarial. They represent the structural nature of the economy. To ignore that does not address the basic structural class issue which we must locate within the capitalist system before we can get people to accommodate and to negotiate rationally. The conflict/adversary nature of discourse is rational in that it accords with the structure of our economy.

SIMPSON: Given that as the reality, we can't win because the other side has all the high cards. We must find a way of breaking out of the current proposition. I simply hope to begin to describe the ways in which people can begin to develop new modes of discourse which will have the long-term effect of bringing much of what is now the preserve of private interests into the public realm. There are ways in which this can be done.

* Peter Warrian, "Trade Unions and the New International Division of Labour", paper prepared for the Boag Foundation Conference on Challenges to Social Democracy in the Eighties and Beyond.

NEW VOICE: In a time of concession bargaining, you are suggesting consensus bargaining. That flies in the face of unions getting power back. How can we explore new avenues now when unions are on the defensive?

SIMPSON: That may be precisely the point.

HEALTH SERVICES
An Anti-Toxin for the Right*

Lee Soderstrom
Department of Economics
McGill University
Montreal, Quebec

MANY OF US HAVE COME TO TAKE government stewardship of health services for granted. We thought it was something untouchable, but of course we were wrong. We were dead wrong. Reagan and Thatcher, Bennett here in B.C., and the Conservatives in Ontario and Alberta are initiating a major attack on government stewardship. The federal Liberals can, at best, be described as doing nothing.

As social democrats we must restate our case. We should review the case for public financing and management of health services. What is the rationale for public stewardship of health services? The basic argument comes down to one

* The article "Health Services: An Anti-Toxin for the Right" is an edited transcription of Prof. Soderstrom's presentation to the discussion group which focused on The People. In his paper "Government Stewardship of Health Services," Prof. Soderstrom elaborates on many of the ideas presented here. The paper is available from the Boag Foundation.

sentence: Public stewardship benefits Canadians from all walks of life. The arguments around public stewardship of health services fall into two classes: technical and ethical. There are implications from these arguments for the left and the right.

The right argues that if the government is involved in our lives they must be making a mess out of it. This knee jerk reaction to any kind of government involvement leads to the proposition that universality is unnecessary, that the state need intervene in the health sector only to help the poor. This is ethically and technically a myth. Unfortunately democratic socialists have contributed to this myth. We focus too much on the benefits to the poor. We do not pay enough attention to the benefits that public stewardship provides for people from all walks of life. Let us remind people that everyone benefits. Universality is necessary.

The *Regina Manifesto* stated:

> With the advance of medical science, the maintenance of a healthy population has become a function for which every civilized community should undertake responsibility. Health services should be made at least as freely available as our educational services today. Under a system which is still mainly one of private enterprise the cost of proper medical care such as the wealthier members of society can afford are at present prohibitive for great masses of the people. A properly organized system of public health services, including medical and dental care, which would stress the prevention rather than the cure of illness should be extended to all our people in both rural and urban areas. this is an enterprise in which dominion, provincial and municipal authorities, as well a medical and dental professions, can co-operate.

It was not just the poor that were envisaged to benefit from socialized health services. It was the great masses of the people. The *Regina Manifesto* makes the case that we need public involvement because many people cannot pay for the services. That is a bit mistaken. Even if everyone could pay, there are still benefits. You can't enjoy the benefits of having a simple financing arrangement unless everyone has the same simple financing arrangement. An efficiently operated system must be available to everyone. There are some things that money per se cannot buy. By engaging in collective activity you can obtain simplicity and efficiency.

We counter the attack from the right by elevating the myth that extra-billing and hospital user fees adversely affect only the poor. That argument is wrong on two counts. Any deterrent affects all people. This is clearly indicted in the technical empirical literature. Where deterrent fees are established, reduction in utilization tends to be equal across all income groups. Concentrating on the effect of deterrent fees on the poor fails to recognize that over-billing and hospital user fees are a direct attack on government steward-ship. A purely economic argument does not address the need for a balanced responsibility between the medical establish-ment and those who represent all of society. Extra-billing and user fees mean that the role of the state in the management of physician services is reduced.

It is a myth that we have to chose between equity and efficiency. The right argues that equity will be inefficient. But the opposite is true. Equity *reduces* the inherent inefficien-cies of multiple insurance companies providing overlapping coverage. The bureaucracy of claim processing is reduced. Cost control is facilitated by public involvement. Govern-ment stewardship enhances effective use of resources, includ-ing the ability of the state to influence the distribution of physician manpower between rural and urban areas. It takes state action to get physicians into rural areas.

Social democrats must defuse the mythology of the right. But we must also rethink our position. The role of the state needs to be improved, not decreased. There may be legiti-mate reasons for reducing the reliance on hospitals but the handling of recent hospital budget cuts has been very poor. We need to improve public decision making through decen-tralization and regional health councils.

We need to rethink our vision of physicians. A key issue for health policy must be to recognize the inordinate influence that physicians have on system performance. The left too often gets hung up on concerns about physicians' incomes. For example, a significant percentage of Quebec youth are not fully innoculated against a common childhood disease. There are over 200 million people in the United States. There are seven million people in Quebec, yet there are more cases of measles in Quebec than in all of the U.S. Measles can be prevented by supplying physicians with free serum and paying them to administer it. This does not happen, because the system worries about paying the doctors more. Instead, the government expends time and money attempting to politicize the doctors to convince them that they should do it anyway. They don't. Over the last ten years the real value of physician fees has fallen. To maintain their incomes, physicians perform more acts, encourage more visits, more surgery, more tests. Encouraging physicians to be preoccupied with fees is counter productive. Increased services mean increased costs, with no consideration for the extent to which the services are necessary or even dangerous. Physicians have an inordinate influence on the system performance and we should give more attention to that.

Physicians shape the performance of the health system in several ways. They act as gatekeepers. As an individual you can't go to the hospital and order triple bypass surgery. The consumer is very dependent on the physician. In our current medical model the medical profession very much influences how we think about and how we approach the whole subject of health and illness. The influence of physicians is reflected in the technological imperative that we have in the health system today. The emphasis is on cure rather than prevention. Our health system discourages people from being concerned about prevention because it emphasizes solutions to health problems after they occur.

The fundamental rationale for public stewardship of health services is that it yields substantial benefits for everyone. Government stewardship can provide simpler financing arrangements. A universal, comprehensive plan providing first dollar coverage without the use of premiums provides assured financial security and humaneness in the provision of services, and administrative efficiency. Public stewardship facilitates better financial control. Cost performance in Canada has been very much better than in the United States. At the beginning of the 1970s both countries spent 7 percent of Gross National Product [GNP] on health services. At the end of the 1970s, Canada continues to spend 7 percent of GNP while the U.S. spends 10 percent. There is no evidence to suggest that Americans are 20-25 percent healthier than Canadians. Waste accounts for the differential.

The technical arguments for public stewardship are clear and well substantiated in the professional literature. The ethical argument stems from the fact that health services, because they influence our capacity to lead a full life, are in a special category. They should be subject to different economic criteria than are other industrial spheres.

DISCUSSION

NEW VOICE: How do we counter the argument that once the poor have been taken care of the rich should have the right to buy anywhere and to decrease the burden on public bureaucracy? The simplicity argument does not extend to the rich. For them one payment a year to a private insurer is simple enough. How do we counter the argument that consumer ignorance is not equal among rich and poor?

SODERSTROM: To the extent that medical diagnosis is increasingly dependent on highly technical procedures, ignorance is spread uniformly across the population. The increased efficiency for hospital accounts receivable procedures of a single insurer outweighs the benefits of simplicity for rich individuals. The existence of any form of private insurance threatens universality. The right to purchase private insurance creates political pressure for a means test which introduces another level of bureaucracy and a demeaning process for some individuals. Any form of means test destroys universality. Once you open the door to private insurance the universal system will erode to a two-tier system very quickly. Social democrats should be addressing the question of a different model. Rather than the current acute care model, which is totally determined by the medical establishment, we should be looking at a preventative system through public health education. Instead of justifying physicians' incomes we should be tackling the idea of physicians on salary. What we have now is not a health system but a sickness system.

NEW VOICE: How do you propose to reduce the influence of the medical establishment?

SODERSTROM: Doctors will have a great deal of power in any system. However, we do ourselves and them a disservice when we concentrate on their income rather than their function. It is apparent from looking at the British model that a private medical system is a drain on the public in a number of ways. The public sector trains the doctors. The public subsidizes the private sector when doctors practice in the private sector.

NEW VOICE: How should a social democratic party approach the problem of maintaining universality?

SODERSTROM: There are some tactical implications. Everyone benefits and we must say that loudly. However, in terms of incremental benefits, some benefit a lot more than others. Some people benefit only indirectly through efficiency and economic stability. The indirect benefits which people don't see and are easily missed are those which should be emphasized.

Do the wealthy believe that they are net incremental beneficiaries of the medicare system? I don't believe they are. We have seriously lost ground by not emphasizing the indirect benefits to the middle income group. Their direct benefits have, in fact, been very small. The major direct beneficiaries are the poor. Tactically, we should be saying very loudly that everyone has a right to adequate medical care, efficiently delivered. We've got two competing rights and as social democrats, we must make a clear choice.

PARTICIPANTS' REPORT
The People

THE ISSUE
Participatory Democracy

Current decision-making processes in society have resulted in broadly felt alienation, a sense of powerlessness, and a low rate of political participation. Socialists have done little to promote effective participation.

DISCUSSION

SOCIALISM MUST INCLUDE A CONCEPT of participatory democracy that will allow citizens to exercise real power and assume responsibility. Societal structures must allow people opportunities to express their co-operative and unselfish inclinations.

The creation of the ability, and the extension of the opportunity, to participate in decision-making structures can only be done through participatory democratic structures, not just in formal political institutions, but throughout society. we must strive to make participatory democracy an inherent and fundamental part of our political and social culture.

The conservative response to political participation emphasizes the enfranchisement of property. Voting privileges and other manifestations of power are linked to the control and distribution of property. The majority has absolute authority. Conservatives assume that opportunities for political participation exist, that people are taught to avail themselves of these opportunities and that not using the available democratic tools reflects a conscious choice. The socialist response presumes that, while citizens should participate in all societal institutions, the promotion of political literacy through institutional structures is a prior responsibility.

The vital link between learning and decision-making must be emphasized. The educative aspects of participatory decision-making can be enhanced by a distribution of power which allows people to see the direct results of their responses. Responsibility and accountability can only be achieved if people are allowed to evaluate and assess their decisions. Counter to the conservatives' elitist presumption that non-participation implies lack of responsibility, social democrats understand that there is a cost of participation for the individual and maintain realistic expectations of participation.

Decision-making opportunities can be increased by greater access to information, the democratization of the delivery of services and the application of participatory democracy in arenas such as the workplace. Participatory democracy involves a shift from parliamentary forms of political decision-making to models based on consensus building.

RECOMMENDATIONS

Models of democracy, implemented outside of parliamentary forums, should acknowledge the trade off between the costs and benefits of participation and give due consideration to economic efficiency. Decision-making power must be legitimate and accessible. Decision-making must produce demonstrable results for people. Different skill and experience levels, as well as cultural, moral and linguistic diversity, must be taken into account. The principle of pluralism must be applied to protect individual and minority interests. Decision-makers must be accountable through participation in evaluation and assessment procedures. Above all, consensus-seeking participatory democracy must be sufficiently flexible to change with people and circumstances.

The end of the industrial era and the emergence of new technologies have increased our ability to communicate. An equal distribution of power, information and communication channels is essential if we hope to survive and progress harmoniously. Democratic socialist organizations should study the use and misuse of technological change, paying particular attention to communication systems which promote participation and democratic accessibility to information. Existing policies and programs should be reviewed and assessed with regard to the principles of participatory democracy.

Socialistic governments should promote participatory democracy in the organizations and structures it controls or influences. Small experimental groups working on the principles of industrial and participatory democracy should be allowed to work on real projects.

THE ISSUE
Social Policy

- provision of adequate and secure income, and the reduction of income inequalities;
- provision of basic social rights relating to health, education, housing, and personal social services (e.g. legal services);
- protection against the adverse effects of industrial life;
- provision of a secure job and a clean and safe environment;
- promotion of social well-being though improved cultural, recreational and other related policies.

DISCUSSION

These issues and their implicit goals have not been attained nor adequately addressed under capitalism. During the postwar era, social policy was not based on the pursuit of people's needs. The social welfare state, in the 1950s and 60s, was inappropriately tied to economic growth as defined by capitalism. As a result, the economic recession of the 1970s and 80s has legitimized the conservative attack on the welfare state.

> The assault on welfarist social policy has harmonized themes concerning the economic, social, political, and moral effects of welfarist social policy. The economic critique . . . has been couched primarily in terms of efficiency. . . . It has been argued that the expenditures devoted to social policy have helped produce growing deficits and have had significant inflationary effects. It claims that government intervention[s] . . . create unanticipated economic consequences which interfere with the optimal operation of markets.
>
> The political critique . . . has attacked the addition of layers of bureaucracy to . . . governments. . . . Governance is less efficient even as citizens feel themselves surrounded by bureaucratic regulation. A social critique . . . has argued that most interventions have refused to examine their real consequences. The claims to create community involvement and democratization . . . mask the advancement of narrow social interests–notably [those of] professionals who see in the elaboration of a social policy apparatus the opportunity for secure positions and a more promising basis for their political power.
>
> Welfare social policy has been attacked as disruptive of community. . . . The state intervenes . . . without sensitivity to . . . preexisting networks. Democratic schemes do not yield democratic results simply through good intentions.
>
> The moral arguments . . . center on statism and the dangers of dependence. Welfarist social policies substitute state initiatives for those of private

citizens and associations. Statism. . . violates the
moral requirements of a free and healthy society.*

Solutions to social policy problems have been hindered,
under capitalism, by the emphasis on individual, rather than
collective, responsibility. Thus, in the face of deteriorating
economic conditions it has been all too easy to blame the
victim and deny the need for the welfare state.

RECOMMENDATIONS

Income Security Program

The two cornerstones of an Income Security Program should
be a commitment to full employment and a commitment to
free and fair collective bargaining.

A full employment policy must be concerned with both the
quality and quantity of jobs. Thus, specific programs are
needed. One group of programs relates to paid work and
includes training and education, childcare, removal of barriers to unionization, and adequate minimum wage. A second
group of programs relates to people who are unable to do
paid work–retirees, the disabled, the unemployed, and people who are parenting. To deal with income security for this
group, we should develop broad universal programs to
replace narrow categorical ones. However, we recognize that
a single universal plan like a guaranteed annual income
cannot cover all these groups of people. For example, the
structure of a public pension plan would be different from a
program providing income for a person who is parenting. The
level of income should provide a decent standard of living
and, in relative terms, promote a narrowing of income
differentials.

Income programs should be funded through progressive
corporate and personal income taxes rather than regressive
specific taxes such as sales taxes and payroll deductions. A

* David Plotke, "The Future of Social Policy: A Response to the Conservative Critique of the Welfare State," paper prepared for the Boag Foundation
Conference on Challenges to Social Democracy in the Eighties and Beyond.

full employment policy would result in additional public revenues through greater corporate and personal tax receipts and the reduction of unemployment insurance, welfare and other indirect social costs.

Basic Health Services
Health services policy must address preventive medical systems as well as providing services for the ill and injured by improving and expanding existing publicly financed and managed health care systems. The system should provide a comprehensive array of services, (e.g., medical, dental, pharmaceutical), efficiently and universally. The delivery system should accommodate working people and working hours through extended or alternate hours of operation. There should be greater access for particular groups of people to particular services. The special needs of women, natives and rural populations must be given consideration. Access to family planning services should be increased. Consideration must also be given to the integration of services. Patients should be better informed and more involved in health care decisions. Finally, public management of the system should include democratically elected regional health care councils.

The health care system should be funded from progressive general income and corporate taxes. Extra-billing by physicians, hospital user fees and health insurance premiums must be prohibited.

This vision of health services reflects principles which should guide the development of other social programs:

Universality
Accessibility
Efficiency
Community Involvement
Progressive Financing

Implementation tactics should make use of education programs which focus on political, as opposed to technical, strategies for reversing the current attack on social services.

Community political action must be supported by credible responses to the current economic, social and moral attacks by conservatives on social services. The credibility of the socialist position depends, partially, on successfully and publicly redefining the narrow capitalistic notions of wealth and wealth creation to include publicly delivered social services. Social policy must come to be seen as a credible means of dealing with economic problems. An income security system would facilitate appropriate adaptation to technological change; a better health care system will make people more productive.

THE ISSUE
Technological Change and Work

Define and create work to ensure full employment based on human needs in an advanced technological society.

DISCUSSION

An industrial strategy which considers the issues of technological change with respect to unions must be developed for Canada.

Existing paid work must be redistributed through mechanisms such as flexible work schedules, more creative options for leisure time, and sabbaticals and early retirement. Unionization of part-time work to improve wages and benefits must be considered. Unions and management must assume joint responsibility for productivity and job distribution. Men and women must be guaranteed equal access to work, and equal pay for work of equal value.

Community work options should be created and extended. Community-based jobs should be capital saving, labour intensive, decentralized enterprises incorporating democratic management principles. Non-exploitive, non-alienating cottage industries and worker co-operatives should be encouraged. Community-based work opportunities would enhance the conserver society, culture, leisure, recreation, education and the arts.

Community work options can be service- or product-oriented enterprises. Decentralized service enterprises could contribute to community housing and transportation. The provision of a wider, more appropriate range of child care services and family centres could be addressed at the community level, as could services for seniors and the handicapped. Multicultural, immigrant, preventive health, and human rights and justice services are most appropriately developed at a community level.

RECOMMENDATIONS

Continuing education, training and retraining, and skills development options are necessary if the problems inherent in providing employment in a high technology society are going to be addressed and solved. There is an obvious need for unions and management to develop flexible apprenticeship programs. Accessible community programs for women, immigrants, youth and the unemployed are also required. Resources must be directed to education at all levels.

II
THE ECONOMY

CAPITALISM, DEMOCRACY AND PATRIARCHY*

Sam Bowles
Professor of Economics
University of Massachusetts
Amherst, Massachusetts
Staff Member
Center for Popular Economics

CAPITALISM HAS FAILED TO DELIVER THE GOODS more spectacularly in the past fifteen years than in any period since the 30s. Paradoxically, this failure coincides with the ideological and political ascendance of capital. This paradox poses a problem for democratic socialists. What is it about the present that explains the ability of capital to dominate the ideological and political arenas? The answer has to do with the distinct nature of the economic crisis of the 1970s' and 80s compared to that

* The article "Capitalism, Democracy and Patriarchy" is an edited transcription of Prof. Bowles' presentation to a plenary session of the conference. It sparked one of the conference's most heated discussions. The article printed here does not do full justice to Prof. Bowles' provocative ideas. They are spelled out more fully in his paper "Wage-Led Growth," which is available from the Boag Foundation.

of the 30s. The 30s gave birth to a vision of economic growth: the Keynesian model.

Neither socialists nor economists have come up with a model which would reconcile our immediate demands for a better standard of living, a safer workplace, etc., with the process of economic growth. Indeed it seems to us, and certainly all the more to political and economic capitalists, that the kinds of things we continue to demand would make the economy work worse rather than better. We are, therefore, roundly rejected by various quite clear-thinking individuals.

The programs for which we fought so hard over such a long period of time now appear to be part of the problem rather than part of the solution. We are faced with a dilemma. The Keynesian model and the conditions of the Great Depression allowed us to unify our vision of the good society with a practical approach to the problem of economic growth. The problems of the 60s, 70s and 80s present us with a trade off. We perceive an essential choice between moral and social concerns—greater equality, greater humanity—and the obvious need for the labour movement and others to come up with a solution to the economic crisis. The two objectives often appear in opposition and socialists are confronted by a kind of benign tolerance. Our social concerns are acknowledged, even appreciated—however, current conventional wisdom says, "It would be nice, but we can't afford it. The economy would collapse or perform even worse."

We are faced with the need for belt tightening, for cuts in social programs in the interests of fostering greater investment and restimulating the growth process. Essentially we have accepted this trade off. Most people on the left have bought the argument that some kind of pulling back from our social objectives is part of the economic reality of the 80s. Much of our ideological and political loss stems from this position.

The idea of a conflict between our moral objectives and our economic objectives is fundamentally false. It is based on an economic model which is fundamentally wrong. Many will recognize this argument as the classic "guns vs. butter" trade off of textbook economics. You can't get something for nothing. There's no such thing as a free lunch. To complain about it is to object to the laws of arithmetic.

The idea of the zero-sum* trade off gives the dismal science its dismal reputation. It assumes full employment and efficient use of resources. For leftists to accept this idea is political suicide. We reject our traditions, which are based on the notion that the capitalist system itself is irrational. Capitalism dictates irrational uses of resources and irrational ways of organizing human productivity toward irrational ends. If we go back to that fundamental notion we can again begin to protest against capitalism.

There are two reasons for optimism. Democracy, as a system which can mobilize people in its defence, has a very good record. The march of democracy is impressive. If our economy is not a zero-sum economy, but is a slack economy in which we do not have to trade off guns vs. butter or consumption vs. investment, and if our political and ideological environment is one in which democracy is a vibrant and mobilizing force, the question arises: is it possible to use a more rational economy? Would a democratic economy be more rational? If the answer to that question is yes, we can once again pursue our moral and economic objectives in a unified way. We can argue for democratization without confessing weakly that there will be trade offs. Socialism can make the economy work better rather than worse.

Our society is organized around two basic games. The games have rules. One game is called capitalism, the other is called democracy. I would add a third called patriarchy or male domination. The capitalist game is played with dollars; the democratic game is played with votes. Until the Great Depression the two games were fundamentally separated. Following the Depression and the Second World War the games overlapped substantially. Socialists have more power when the game is played with votes than when it is played with dollars. The fundamental thrust of any socialist eco-

---

* A situation in the theory of games in which the gains and losses of the players must sum to zero. When there are two players, gains by one must be identical to losses by the other. Players are in pure conflict.

nomic strategy should be to shift the terrain of debate towards the game that is played with votes.

The Alligator Strategy

Alligators lie in a watering hole with just their eyes sticking out. The water buffaloes come down to drink. The water buffalo puts its foot in the water. The alligator grabs the foot. A tremendous struggle ensues. The water buffalo is defenceless if pulled into the water. The alligator, if pulled up onto the land, will get stomped.

That's the game we're playing. We have to pull capital into the water. We have to understand that there are some terrains on which we are much stronger than others.

DISCUSSION*

NEW VOICE: I appreciate your adding **patriarchy** to your list. I would like you not to ignore it.

NEW VOICE: The phrase **"zero-sum"** comes from **Lester Thurow** and I think you have missed his point and consequently haven't addressed it. Although he would acknowledge that there is a sense in which capitalism does not support rationality, there is a sense in which the unemployment generated under capitalism is rational. It is rational in the same way that Marx recognized the reserve army of labour as being rational. With the reserve army of labour, the distribution of income is different than it would be without the reserve army of labour. Unemployment is a response to the problem. It is an attempt to solve a problem with a particular distribution of income. It is true that we can solve a number of problems by moving to full employment, but the distribution of the benefits and the costs of production will

* Prof. Bowles' answers follow a series of comments and questions which were solicited from the plenary audience. Words in bold face indicate major concepts introduced into the discussion.

be different under that system than under a system with large amounts of unemployment. That, in my opinion, is the point that Thurow is trying to make. The trade off is a distributional one. Who is shouldering the majority of the costs? Who is reaping the majority of the benefits, on an individual basis? He concludes that we fail because we try to tackle social policy in the political arena and have left economic policy and economic power alone. His solution is to tackle economic issues as you address social issues. They can't be separated. Therefore, he certainly wouldn't agree with your conclusion, although he wouldn't reject it. We've got to fight the battle on the political front. He would say it must also be fought in an arena which we have neglected, that is, the productive front.

NEW VOICE: Putting the emphasis on the **slack economy** is essentially the Keynesian point of view. Emphasizing resources lying idle and saying that we can have more guns and more butter is what Keynes said and he was right. But in the minds of the electorate that is now discredited. I question whether you will get far pushing that line of thought today. You are trying to counter a right wing point of view held by a lot of the electorate. If you push for higher wages the response will be, we live in a competitive world, we have to compete, especially with the Third World. Your **wage-led growth strategy** flies in the face of the conventional wisdom and while we may disagree, it is an issue we have to address.

NEW VOICE: A high wage theory is music to the ears of any trade unionist, particularly if it is conjoint with a moral appeal that our excessive wage demands serve a higher purpose. There are two issues I would like to put to you. How do we deal with the very devastating issue, for trade unions, of **capital mobility**? Are there **limits to growth** in consumption that we can or want to discuss from a left perspective, without accepting the zero-sum theory?

NEW VOICE: How much of the decline in the impact of the left might be traced to the fact that it refused to take **inflation** as a serious problem whereas the population sees it as a very serious problem?

NEW VOICE: To what extent is current **inflation** a function of 30 years of the non-productive arms race in the world?

NEW VOICE: The observation that democracy and capitalism are perhaps incompatible is not unique. It is, in fact, the fundamental basis of the neo-conservative critique of the welfare state which contends that our economic problems, namely inflation, are a result of **too much democracy.** What kinds of dilemmas do the parallels with the right critique of the welfare state pose for democratic socialists, ideologically and economically?

NEW VOICE: The mutual exclusivity of the capitalist game and the democratic game is pretty theoretical. What may once have been in separate spheres are now in the same sphere. Capital buys votes. That's something I have experienced personally. I'm in a low-rent party. I had an equal and democratic opportunity to buy T.V. ads and the equal and democratic opportunity to pay for them.

NEW VOICE: It's easy to deride private investment on the grounds that you have investment decisions made by profit hungry capitalists and urge instead that investment decisions be made by government. But suppose that government consists of faceless bureaucrats given their instructions by vote-hungry politicians. Would one want to argue that government should determine all investment decisions?

NEW VOICE: To the extent that there is slack in the economy and we are making the Keynesian case that we can have more, I agree with your argument. Peter Warrian just loved your paper. He came up to me, an advocate of Incomes Policy, and chortled. However, I put to you that you are fundamentally wrong. I don't want to beat around the bush. The democratic left will regain credibility when it can address the issue of **trade offs.** We fail because we have not been able to determine what the split between public sector and private sector, the split between consumption now and investment in the future, should be. Whether we say it as a left wing political party, as trade unionists, or as public managers of public corporations, goddam it, these trade offs exist. If you want to give us a nirvana view of the left and say we can have it all, you're wrong. I would like you to say why I'm wrong.

NEW VOICE: Could you comment on how we could identify the real trade offs? The phony trade off which you have identified and we have recognized is not correct because we are not on a **production** possibility front. Perhaps there are real trade offs, not only in terms of internal income distribution, but on a global scale. This gets us to the question of **inflation** caused by OPEC and financing the Vietnam War without tax increases which should have meant at least a short-term cut in real income.

PROF. BOWLES:
(Zero-Sum/Lester Thurow) Lester Thurow is an egalitarian. He has no part whatsoever with the conservative ideologies which are associated with the use of the zero-sum idea. The title of his book and some of the analysis was unfortunate and has certainly been picked up to justify belt tightening by workers in the interest of prosperity. Lester Thurow is not part of that and I am glad to have it pointed out.

(The slack economy) The Keynesian model is not an adequate description of the economic crisis we are now facing. It is a relatively more adequate description of the last crisis, the Great Depression. Why are we in a slack economy if the fundamental nature of the situation now is not Keynesian? The idea that we have a slack economy implies that there is waste. There are two kinds of waste in the economy: demand side and supply side.

Demand side waste was emphasized by Keynes. Today's level of unemployment and capacity underutilization indicates a tremendous amount of demand side waste. But to point to this as evidence for the correctness of the Keynesian model would be false and I think very dangerous for socialists. The current economic crisis broke under conditions of very high capacity utilization and very high employment. We see the beginning of the economic crisis, in virtually all of the advanced capitalist countries, in the late 60s, well before OPEC. This was a period of very high investment, very high demand, very high employment. The nature of the crisis we are now in is not fundamentally Keynesian. The policies which have been pursued in most countries since about 1973, and in the United States since 1979, have recreated the Keynesian condition. The problem of demand for goods and services has become the fundamental problem facing capital today. But if we were to act on this, we would soon discover that there are other problems equally important and more pressing. We would simply recreate the conditions which brought about the crisis in the first place. We cannot go with the Keynesian model.

The other kind of waste is supply side waste. Every Marxist economist must be a supply side economist. All that supply side economists say is that there is waste in the economy, in the way things are produced in the production system itself. It's perfectly obvious. Anybody who believes that capitalism is an irrational system knows that there are problems on the supply side. There is waste on the supply side as well as on the demand side. What kind of waste? Waste in the way the labour process is controlled and waste in the way work is regulated through management supervision. There is waste in what is produced, to the extent that what is profitable is not useful, either because of environmental spillover effects or for other reasons. We owe a debt of gratitude to supply side economics for the criticism of the inadequacy of the Keynesian model and for pointing to the system of production itself. Of course the difference between us and them, or at least between me and them, is that they finger the government as the culprit in supply side waste and I would point to capitalism. But why quibble over small differences.

I am not advocating a return to the Keynesian model. I say this very sadly. If we were in a Keynesian world, we would all be much happier. Probably many people in this room would be in power. As long as it was true in the short run to say that the problem with capitalism was simply that workers weren't getting enough money and that by simply paying workers more you could make capitalism work better, there was a perfect program for the labour movement. We are in a crisis now which took place, not because the working class was too weak as it was in the 1920s, but because, in a sense, the working class was too strong. This is what I assert happened in Europe and in the other countries of the advanced capitalist world. In the late 60s and early 70s, there was a crisis of capital which took place precisely because workers and other popular groups had successfully used the demo-cratic processes of the state to put a squeeze on capital. That's our dilemma. We can't argue that more power to workers and popular groups is going to make capitalism work better if we understand the crisis in that way. We are therefore faced with a choice of either returning power to the capitalist class because, after all, a prosperous capitalism is better than a limping capitalism, if you have to have capitalism at all, or of changing the rules so that by pursuing the very same objectives, or new objectives, the economy can work better.

(Rational Unemployment) Unemployment does have a function within the capitalist system – it keeps workers on the defensive. If you get rid of unemployment you change the distributional picture. That's precisely what happened in the 60s. At that point there is a crisis. Do you then say, let's have more unemployment so that capitalism can regain its power. Or do you say, it would be better to pursue a full employment economy and a rapidly growing economy? Can we dispense with anxiety and fear as the basis on which this economy is run? That is the question which is now posed to us. We don't have the easy solutions of the Keynesian model. Now we have to think about changing the rules, and changing the rules means talking about socialism. It means finding a new way to motivate work, and to organize production and investment decisions. Unless we are willing to take that step forward, we are going to lose, as we have been losing for the last ten years. That is why a conference of this nature, which is to a certain extent visionary in its outlook, is absolutely what we need.

I used to be one of those carping critics of utopianism because I thought it was idealistic. Training as a Marxist can warp the mind. I think that I was just dead wrong. We need to think about a totally new agenda. The labour movement and leftists gave up visionary thinking partly because of the success of the Keynesian model. They did so well with dollars and cents issues. I agree with Lester Thurow that if you do not change the rules you are operating in a zero-sum environment. Perhaps he doesn't think it's possible or perhaps he doesn't want to be advocating that position in the present political environment. I think it is possible. I think we must advocate changing the rules to eliminate some of the irrationality of capitalism which will then provide the basis for what was described as the unrealistic idea that we can have more of everything.

(Trade offs) A situation which is as free of trade offs as the present simply bespeaks a level of irrationality which is unusual even in the history of capitalism. If we were to move to a more rational social policy, if we were even to be in the situation in which the Swedish labour movement found itself in the late 60s and early 70s for example, we would have to say, of course there are trade offs. As you move from a relatively less rational use of resources to the full use of resources you face trade offs and they are very hard ones. The left has to deal with that. The left has not been very good about identifying what the real trade offs are and then talking about them in an intellectual and disciplined manner. The trade off is not between consumption and investment. The difficult trade offs are between centralization and decentralization, majority and minority rights, and internationalism and protectionism. The tendency to say that in the best of all possible worlds we won't have to deal with these trade offs is not particularly helpful.

(Equalization of wages) A wage-led growth strategy implies raising wages from the bottom up. The political rationale is fairly obvious. A wage structure as unequal as that in the

United States or Canada is one of the many economic bases for the racism, sexism and credentialism which exist between workers. It saps the unity of the movements of which we are a part. Obviously, equalizing wages in the long run is a necessary part of a more fair society and a more unified movement. YAWN. How many times have we said that. Of course, it's true, but what's good about it economically? It is the best industrial policy a society such as Canada or the United States could have today. It would drive out all firms which can't hack paying workers eight or ten dollars an hour but, in fact, have to pay them three or four dollars an hour in order to make a profit. Given the present distribution of political forces, raising wages from the bottom up would be tremendously egalitarian. That's my idea of industrial policy at the present time. In conjunction with a full development policy, it would have very large effects on productivity. Notice, the productivity effects of this would simply be the elimination of unproductive firms. You may say, this is not socialism and I think we all would agree, but it is the kind of thing which can be advocated in the name of equality and in the name of increasing the economic performance of the economy which does not involve giving power to some investment board dominated by capitalism. It is a policy which would help to unify the left rather than dividing it. If labour's primary loyalty is to its membership, it may not be overly enthusiastic about the idea of equalizing wages from the bottom up. Obviously, equalizing wages from the bottom up does not mean that you first fight for higher wages in the relatively high-wage sectors. That is a problem we have to face.

(Capital Flight) If we mean it when we say that capitalism is a system based on exploitation, then moving toward socialism or even toward a more democratic society means reducing exploitation. We mean that we are going to threaten the privileges of capital. We mean that we are going to lower the profit rate. In the long run there is no way around that. Our analysis of capitalism as an exploitative system leads us to the conclusion that we will ultimately threaten the privileges of capital. Obviously, the way the game is played, capital can go wherever it wants. We come up against a conflict between the privileges of capitalism to locate wherever it pleases and the sovereignty of a society to make decisions about its economic future. In the alligator strategy, choosing the terrain of capital flight and posing the opposition between democracy and profitability is not necessarily a battle we can win. But it is one which we are more likely to win than almost any other battle I can think of. I would argue that the issue of capital flight is if not *the* most important then *one* of the most important economic issues facing us. I would suggest we argue this, not on narrow grounds of job preservation, because those demands tend to be corporatist and to divide workers one from another, but on the high ground. Unless we control capital flight, we essentially surrender the sovereignty of the society and the democratic processes to the mobility of capital. In 1933, Keynes argued for limiting the degree of economic openness because of the necessity of each society experimenting to find solutions to the economic crisis they were then facing.

(Limits to Growth) The problem of productivity in the economy is very important. The left cannot make headway as a mass movement unless it addresses the problem of productivity and economic performance. I do not believe that we should produce more new goods and services or more of what we are already producing. I don't even know if we should produce more or what we would produce if we had control over the allocation of resources. The growth of productivity allows the expansion of free time which is a very major issue. It must be taken up by the left, not just on narrow grounds of sharing the unemployment, so to speak. If we could restimulate productivity growth, we could cut the work week quite radically within a generation. This would have the effect of allowing a more vibrant, active life in other spheres of the society. It would allow for more active political engagement. Oscar Wilde said the problem with socialism is that it would take too many evenings. And yes, weekends as well. This is literally true. A socialist society is a more politicized, a more mobilized, less passive society. It requires more free time. In other terms, if we are ever going to **fundamentally change relations between men and women** in families, we have to have the possibility of sharing child rearing. You can't move toward sharing child rearing when you have both unequal wages and the necessity of full-time work. The bias against moving in that direction is extreme. The reduction of work hours and the equalization of wages would revive the possibility of a real democratic culture and would provide the economic basis, if not the political impetus, for a more sustained attack on the sexual division of labour within the family. The reduction in work hours would have to be coupled with increasing expenditures for cultural and recreational activities.

(Inflation) The left has suffered terribly by not dealing with inflation. Until the 70s it was the case that all workers benefited from full employment. All workers were better off during a business cycle expansion – those employed and those who would otherwise have been unemployed. In the 70s, a new phenomenon developed. Workers who had jobs did better during contractions than during expansions. Sound strange? Think about inflation! In 1979, which was the peak of a business cycle in the United States, industrial workers lost 4.5 percent in real wages. That is the largest single decline in real wages in one year that has occurred since they have collected the data. That was the peak of the business cycle. That was the time in which you would have thought that the workers would have been most powerful. Those who had jobs lost terribly. Those who didn't lose their jobs did much better in the mini-recession of the next year. You have to ask, who has job security and who doesn't? Middle-aged, white, male, trade union members are less likely to be vulnerable to a cyclical recession than young, old, female, black, chicano, native and unorganized workers. There is a division between these two groups of workers. Those who don't have a job benefit from the expansion of the cycle, from a full employment policy. As long as the left does not support price controls, you will find a very large number of white, male, workers who have job security opposing full employment. Sometimes the left views workers who don't support full employment as irrational. They're not irrational at all, they just know the economic situation better than we do. We need an inflation policy and I think it should be price controls.

I don't think inflation has anything to do with the arms race. The left and the peace movement have made a lot out of the inflation-military connection. It is a powerful argument but in view of the fact that military spending has been very popular when it has been undertaken and, therefore, people are very happy to pay taxes for it, I don't think you can make that argument. Of all the things which explain the fundamental basis of the inflation of the 70s, I would not place military spending very high on the list. For one reason, military spending in the 70s was much lower than it had been in any other decade of the postwar period. I speak somewhat cavalierly about this. It is a serious issue and I don't mean to suggest that it is not an open question. It is something which should be actively debated and researched.

(Too much democracy) The right could be right. They could be correct from their standpoint. The Trilateral Commission of 1975 was quite perceptive. They understood that the democratic process was making inroads on capital and that it was a problem. There are two ways to respond: "Oh no it's not true; there's nothing wrong with democracy," or, "Oh yes it's true, there's nothing wrong with democracy." As a metaphor, a broad brush picture, the right is on target about what happened in the 60s and 70s. For the first time in history, capitalists are openly arguing against democratic processes. The left, which in the postwar period has ironically been positioned as being somehow undemocratic, is being handed an issue on a silver platter. The capitalist class is saying, we invite you to contest us on the issue of democracy versus profit. Ironically, we are saying no. We say we would still prefer to fight on the basis of equality. But why not democracy versus profit? It's a great issue! It comes very naturally to the socialist tradition and it is an issue which, in the long run, capitalists can't win.

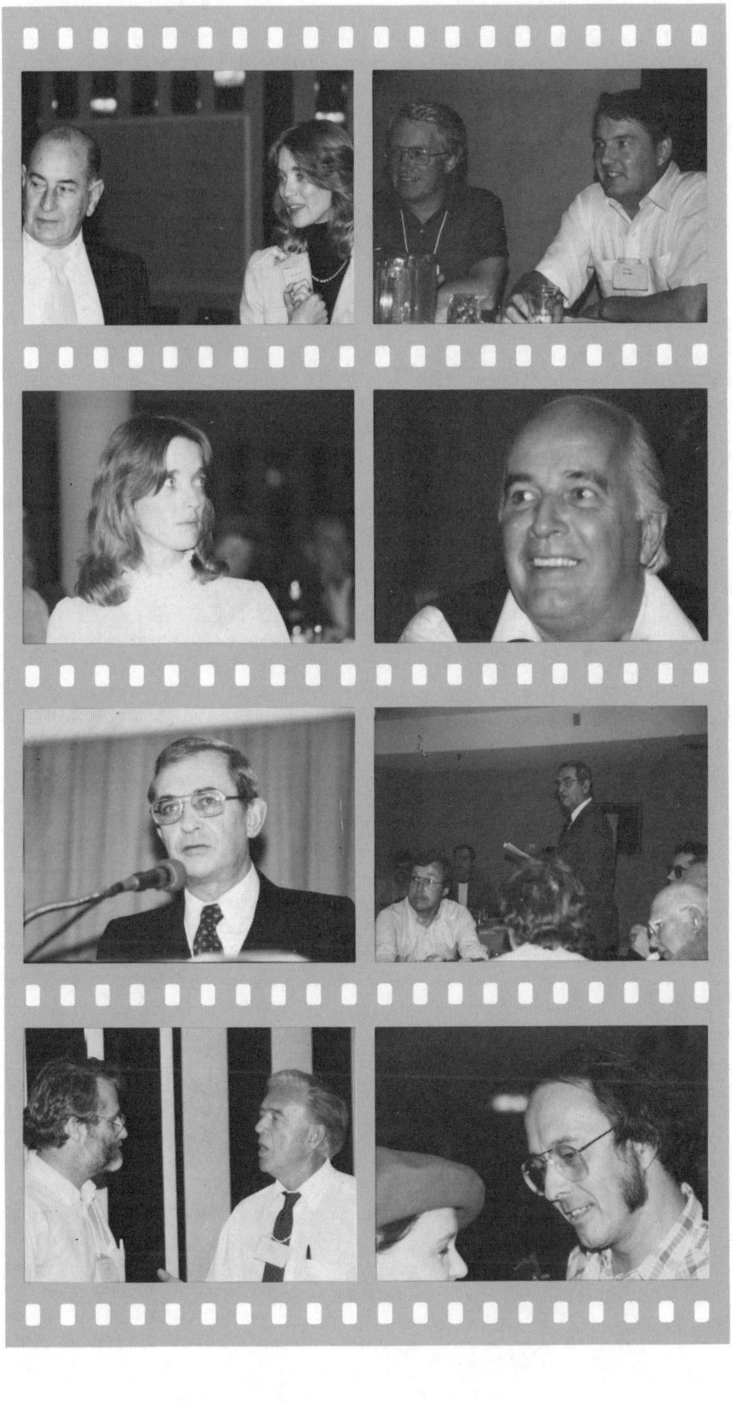

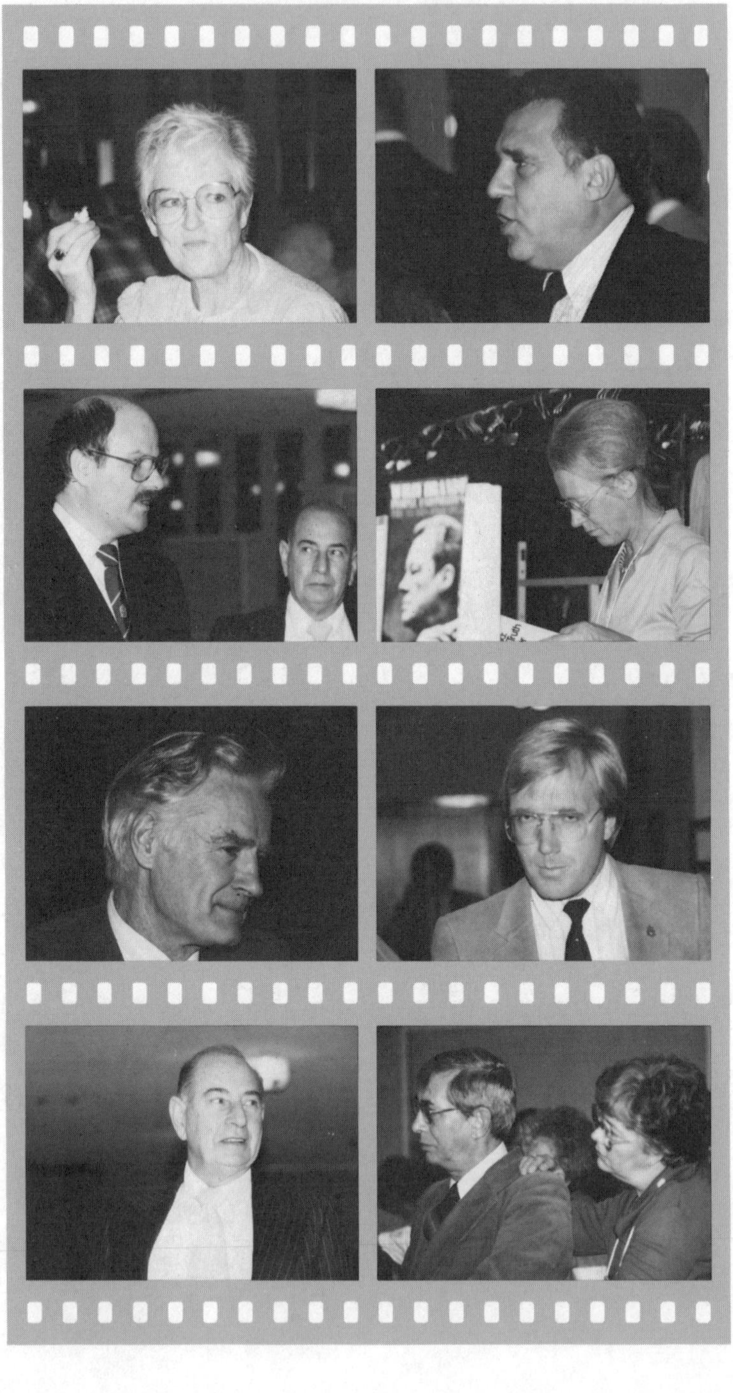

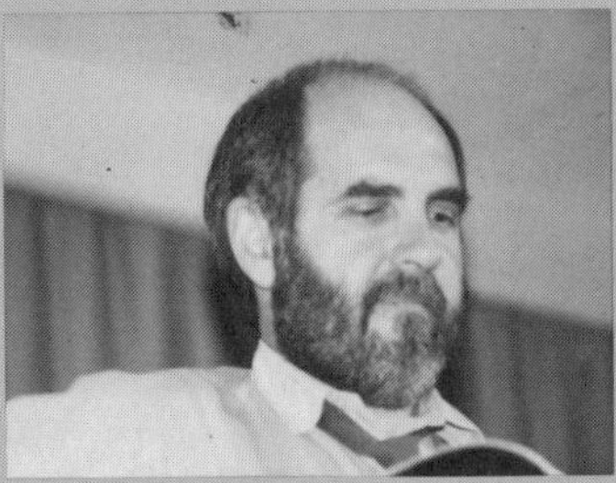
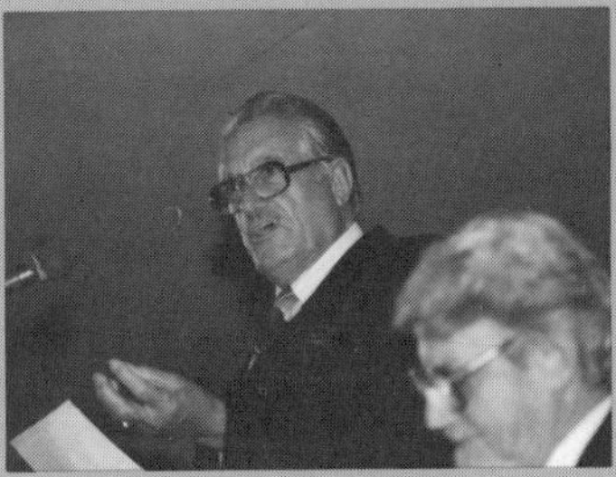
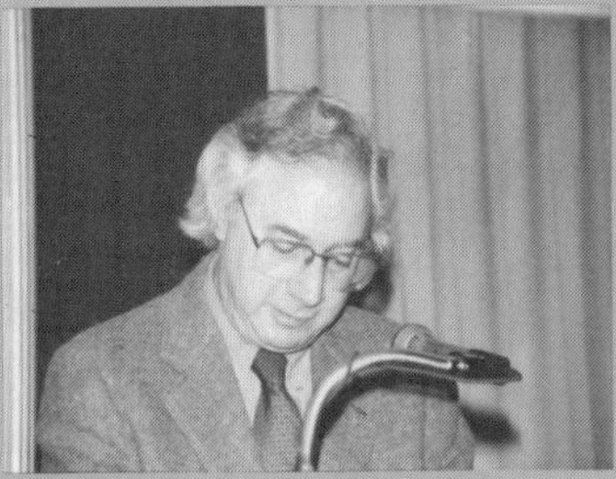
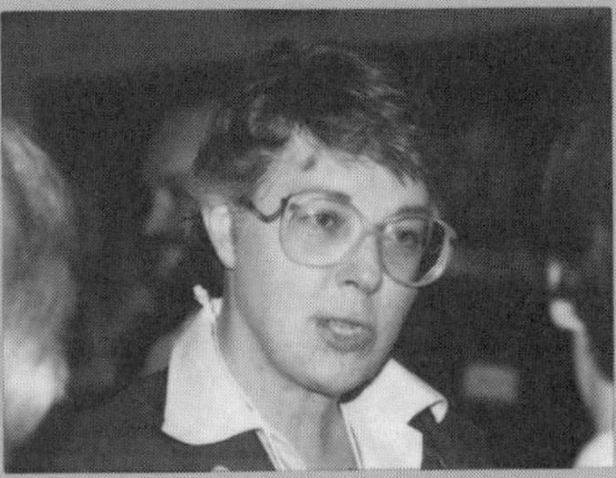
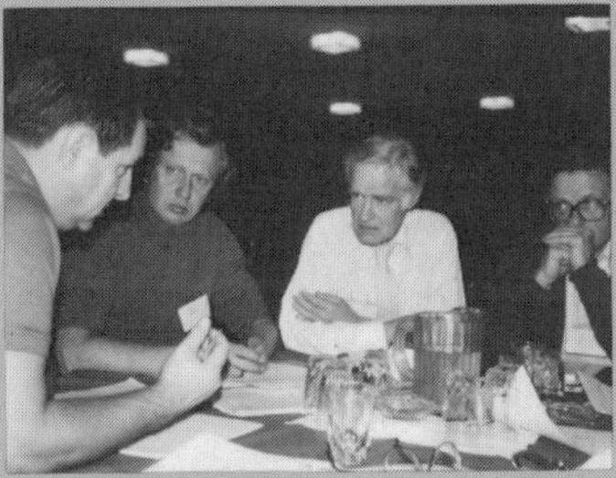
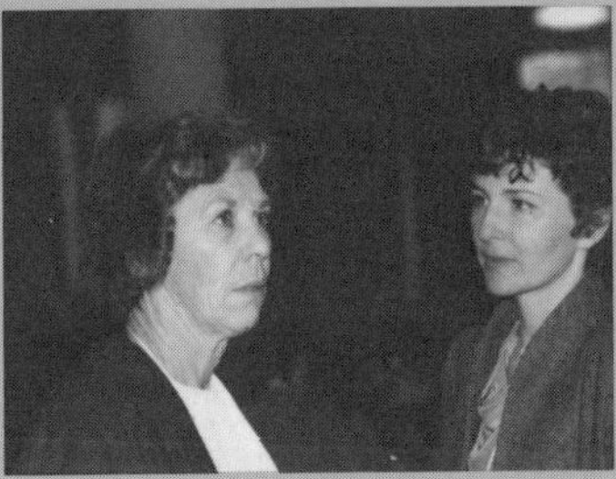
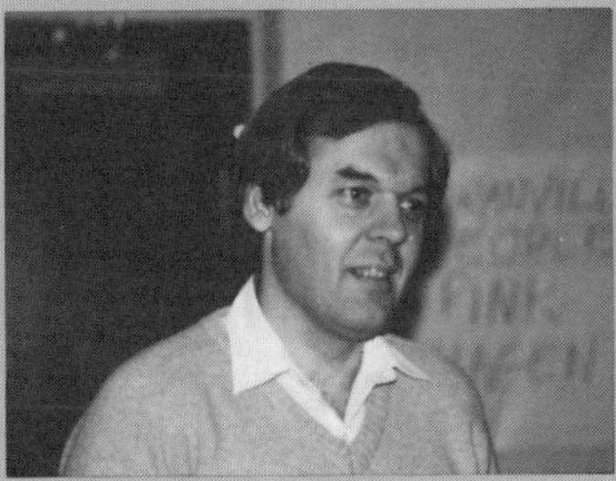
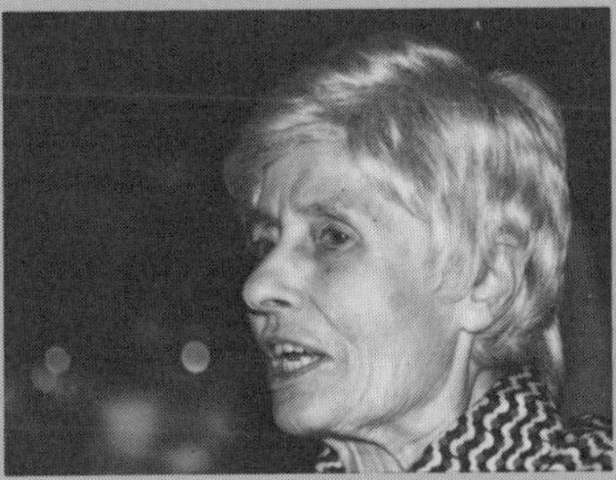

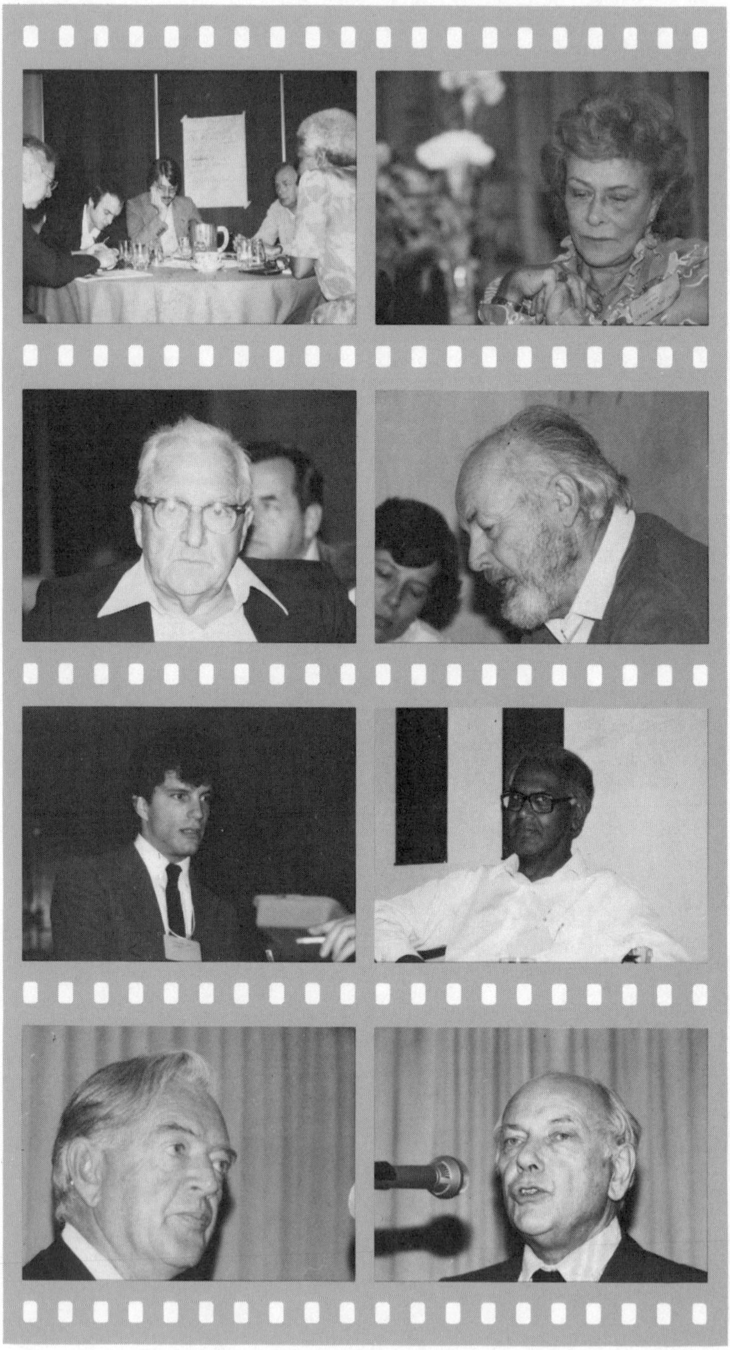

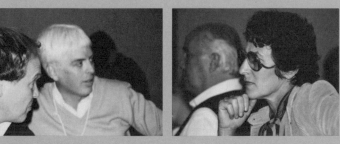

RECASTING ECONOMIC AND SOCIAL POLICIES*

David Plotke
Department of Sociology
University of California
Berkeley, California

I AM AN AMERICAN and although I attempt to consider and understand the differences between the United States and Canada, listening to the participants at this conference has made me realize how much my ideas are shaped by the American experience. There isn't a social democratic impulse in American national politics that amounts to very much. There is a strong liberal impulse that, superficially, can look very similar in terms of programs and formula. In fact, it can look identical. But progressive, egalitarian social policy in the United States has had to be justified not in terms of a normative standard for society, but in relation to economic

*The article "Recasting Economic and Social Policies" is an edited transcription of Prof. Plotke's presentation to a discussion group focusing on The Economy. In his paper "The Future of Social Policy," Prof. Plotke elaborates on many of the ideas presented here. The paper is available from the Boag Foundation.

growth. In the United States, you have to show how social policy is related to an economic growth process.

During the last ten to fifteen years we have seen a dramatic shift in the politics of social policy. Formerly the province of liberals, social policy is now an initiative of the right. Fifteen years ago, at a conference like this, our discussion would be about how to improve social policy measures, how to improve redistributive or egalitarian measures, how to look at where they are lacking, where they are bureaucratic, where they prevent constituencies from getting organized and mobilized. We would be the loyal, sometimes a little disloyal, opposition. Now, we find ourselves in a situation where we are compelled to justify and defend social welfare measures that we weren't necessarily firmly in support of the first time around in order to protect them from assault. That defensive posture seems to be characteristic of what one has to do in Canada. It is certainly what one has to do in the United Kingdom. It is true in the United States and is becoming true elsewhere in the world.

When one argues social policy politically, it is not sufficient to say that some people are suffering because of cutbacks. As a flatly political condition, it can no longer be assumed that the goals of social policy ought to be egalitarian. That is not a sufficient political response to the relatively coherent and integrated conservative attack on social welfare policy.

The conservative critique of welfare policy has economic, political and moral dimensions. It is not just a crude right wing demand that poor people be made to suffer. Because this critique has won wide popular respect, it is not politically sufficient simply to try to unmask it. Social democrats cannot just say that the current conservative policies only serve the rich. This stance has not been successful and is not going to be successful because it does not deal with the fundamental points the critique has made.

ELEMENTS OF THE CONSERVATIVE CRITIQUE
OF WELFARE POLICY

Economic Critique

Social policy expenditures have helped produce growing deficits and have had significant inflationary effects. This argument refuses to accept the idea that the positive economic consequences of social programs, in terms of sustaining demand, compensate for some of the problems they create. The far right has insisted that many social policy measures are economically inefficient because they interfere with the operation of the market. This is traditional, far right, free market rhetoric. This argument has yet to be made successfully to the mass of the population. Voters do not yet believe that we should get rid of minimum wage laws because they keep young people unemployed. But the argument has been more influential among policy making elites than liberal and left analysts would like to admit.

Political Critique

The right argues that welfare policy and social policy have added layers of bureaucracy to government, making it more expensive and inefficient to run. Secondly, they argue that social policy and the legitimization of demands make it harder to govern society because you have more special interests groups demanding more things. Conservative rhetoric recites a constant litany of complaints about groups assaulting the government with demands and concludes that all the turmoil adds up to a situation which cannot be governed effectively.

Social Critique

Conservatives make a "new class" argument about social policy. They say that social measures, purported to serve broad population constituencies, in fact benefit elites which get positions in the bureaucracies that are intended to serve the people. The goals of the policies have not been reached. Instead the policies have served as self-employment and self-improvement mechanisms for new waves of professionals.

They argue that social policies have destroyed communities. This is a powerful populist argument in the United States. Federal social policies have had the effect of interfering in communities, disrupting community associations, and destroying local and residential networks in favour of state paternalism and state bureaucratic control.

Moral Critique

The right points to the consequences of dependence on the state. Welfare measures are couched in terms of helping people but what they typically end up doing is creating client populations who became permanently dependent on the state. That connects back to the social argument. A demoralized client group fits nicely with the needs of new professionals for permanent jobs.

You have to go very far to the right in the United States to hear people conclude from these criticisms that the welfare system should be dismantled. Much more commonly the conclusion is that social policy and social welfare should return to the point it was at in 1936-37. We should have social security and unemployment insurance but no new programs deserve to be brought into place. Far right conservatives, unreconciled even to the most basic kinds of social welfare, are unable to argue their point of view publicly, but they have it in their agenda.

These arguments, taken together, have registered a series of victories against liberal and social democratic arguments in the United States. Although it hasn't happened yet, this group of arguments verges on becoming a new kind of common sense in American politics. It threatens to replace the common sense of the 60s and 70s, when it was assumed to be the obligation of the state to engage in social policy measures to try to remedy social problems.

Some of the conservative arguments are uneasily close to the arguments that the left made about social welfare policy in the 60s and 70s. There is overlap, for example, in the bureaucracy argument. Conservatives attack social policy for setting up bureaucratic structures. Some of us who actively criticized these structures don't want to become caught in the position of seeming to defend them as they were set up and implemented in the United States. It is a tricky task to defend the programs without appearing to endorse the form in which many of them were developed.

In the United States, the notion that welfare policies create client populations is frequently loaded with racial connotations. Welfare policies support blacks and hispanics as dependents and contain an undeniable racial component. The truth, however, is that within black and hispanic communities there is a great deal of ambivalence about welfare programs over precisely the same issue. The programs do not move people out of welfare situations. They do not have the effect of actually changing people's situations. The left is left defending minimal welfare programs without completely denying the germs of truth present in the conservative critique.

The conservative critique has slammed economic and social policy back together in a very abrupt way. In the 60s and 70s, economic and social policy could be quite separate because the assumption was that effective economic policy tools existed to produce sustained growth. When growth is seen as unproblematic, we can turn to social policy and try to deal with what's marginal. For example, in the United States, employment training programs are seen as social policy programs which deal with marginal groups. They are not seen as an economic policy which would significantly affect the operation of the economic mechanism. The conservative critique has essentially denied that separation. The thrust of its economic argument has been that social policy programs have to be subordinated to the market, that they have been socially and economically inefficient and that separation can no longer be tolerated.

It is incumbent upon social democrats to reconnect social policy programs and economic policy arguments in a new way. We can no longer take economic prosperity for granted. We can make serious arguments about why social policy measures are economically desirable. They are not detrimental and they are going to become increasingly essential to any kind of balanced, reasonably democratic, economic growth.

That is not an argument to abandon attempts to justify social policy measure on egalitarian or humanitarian grounds. It is necessary and possible to make an argument about social policy in relation to the economy that insists that an expanded set of social policy and welfare measures can contribute to economic growth and prosperity in the coming period.

DISCUSSION

NEW VOICE: Thank you for stressing the importance of the differences between the Canadian and American contexts. Canada has an unfortunate tradition in that many "innovations" that manifest themselves in the United States appear in Canada a decade later. In the current economic climate many of the American expressions of right wing philosophy impinge on social policy in Canada today.

NEW VOICE: One of the problems of leftist social policy, and the reason why the right seems to have the advantage, is that for the last ten years the left has been in headlong retreat. We have bought into conservative arguments. We agree that because the economy is not expanding rapidly we, therefore, cannot afford redistributive programs. That argument is fallacious. Even with the last recession, our level of prosperity is unprecedented. Concomitant with this high level of prosperity, there also exists an increasingly inequitable distribution of wealth and income. Discussing social policy without reference to the distribution of wealth and income is somewhat akin to discussing the lumber industry without reference to forests.

A finer discrimination between transfer and so-called fringe welfare programs should be made. Transfer programs, primarily social security, benefit the middle class; fringe programs–if you want to call 20-35 percent of the people fringe–address the recognized pluralistic nature of our society. I think you give too much credence to the idea of structural welfare dependency. Welfare rates are too inadequate to engender anything but absolute despair and despondence among the recipients. The substance rather than the structure is calculated to defeat any individual initiative to raise oneself above a substandard level of existence. In rejecting the conservative argument, we should refer to detailed and rigorous academic work done on distributive programs, particularly in Europe. Organization for Economic Co-operation and Development [OECD] studies have shown an almost direct correlation between coefficients measuring income distribution and rates of economic growth. Part of the reason we are stagnating is because there is not enough demand. Part of the reason there is not enough demand is that there is too much money concentrated at the upper end of the scale. A more equitable distribution would put consumer dollars in the hands of people at the lower end, people who would immediately go out and spend their money. The economic principle which states that later spent dollars have a lower circulatory value than earlier spent dollars is a powerful argument on behalf of social programs.

NEW VOICE: I find it mindboggling that the left is not attacking these issues politically. They are tailor made for us. Some of the right's moral arguments are so bankrupt they don't even deserve recognition. The same arguments were used when The Poor Laws were introduced in England. Welfare will destroy individual initiatives; people should have an incentive to save; welfare is a family responsibility; these people are probably sinners and should be made to suffer on earth. We should treat these arguments with contempt. There is strong evidence that the industrial transformation which we are undergoing will restructure the labour force. The largest new employment sectors will be poorly paid, unorganized and exploited. It is the challenge of the left to draw up policies, beyond minimum wage policies, of wage supplementation. There is an element of merit to the conservative critique that social programs have tended to benefit a public sector elite. In B.C. we have too damn many social workers and not enough money for clients. We should examine our automatic, knee-jerk reaction against anything that has to do with attacking public sector workers. There is a whole range of tactics we could use. For example, tax welfare for the upper classes is inextricably linked to transfer payment welfare. Tax welfare guarantees that we do not have sufficient funds to adequately finance social programs. Ideally, all social programs, if they are truly redistributive, should be self-financing. They should not be inflationary or cause deficits.

PLOTKE: I assume that we all are in favour of redistributive measures, but in the United States that remains something for which one has to argue. That may be a bad thing, but the political response cannot be simply to insist that we're right to want to redistribute income. It is a morally correct posture, but it is not politically adequate. I strongly disagree with the idea that we should treat conservative arguments with contempt and by acting contemptuously show that they are wrong. The conservative arguments have won broad popular acceptance. In practice, to treat the arguments with contempt amounts to treating the people who make and accept them with contempt. Talk of contempt and moral bankruptcy is a good argument for drawing together the hard core of people on the left. It's a signal that we who hold these views in contempt should unite and assert our identity. However, you must actually engage the arguments politically. We have to understand why people take these arguments seriously and be prepared to explain to people why they are wrong. It's just not true that the only criticism that people in welfare dependent communities have of welfare is that the rates are too low. There are really serious problems with some programs. You have to deal with the arguments with some response other than contempt.

NEW VOICE: I am also from the United States. Today the attitude of the majority of people toward government differs markedly from the 1930s and 40s. The New Deal was seen as defending and sustaining family, neighbourhood and community institutions. Rural electrification was viewed as a tremendous aid to people in rural settings. Social security was seen as a strong family program which gave dignity to older people in their retirement years. For a long time liberals in the Democratic party were identified with support for neighbourhoods, families and communities. Today that is not the case. The right is seen as the group supporting that constituency. Liberal democratic policies are now seen as very threatening. Busing has inflamed a passionate debate about its effect on neighbourhoods and families. Whatever one's position on integration, it is hard to escape the fact that the effect has been to alienate a tremendous constituency of the liberal left. That personal experience spills over and softens liberal resistance to the right. Similarly, environmental and occupational health and safety regulations introduced in the late 60s and 70s were implemented in such a way that they had a tougher effect on small businesses which were integrated into communities. The big multinational corporations could absorb the costs and pass them on to consumers; they could go to another country or move their money into interim assets and just close down plants for a while. Neighbourhood and community enterprises, which usually identified with liberal policies, were shut down. Whether or not the small businesses went under because of regulatory efforts put forward by the government, those efforts were perceived as a threat. The left has lost its identification with community, perhaps not forever, but we are on the defensive while the right is gaining organizationally on many fronts. The Equal Rights Amendment [ERA] is another example. The merits of ERA are incontrovertible but the right was able to turn it into an issue which threatened families, neighbourhoods and communities. How can we frame social and economic policy in a way which is not threatening to the institutions of our society but supportive of them?

NEW VOICE: It is entirely appropriate to discuss the welfare state within the context of the economy. The welfare state is very much an economic policy. However, it is much less a policy of the left than we like to think. It is important to distinguish between the legitimation and the ideology of the welfare state and the real economic reasons for having it in the first place. In formulating a response to arguments which would dismantle the welfare state, we must respond to more than the legitimation argument. This is what we do when we take the right's critique seriously without looking at the underlying structure. We, on the left, want to have more humane policies. We have accepted the welfare state as a way of going about that in lieu of fundamental economic changes. That is not a criticism. I am not mad at us for doing that. We were in a box and that was really all we could do. But nonetheless it has deflected us from seeing that the real task is to fundamentally change the economy. Historically, the welfare state is linked to the development of large corporations and to their need for a stable and reserve labour force. A corporate economy needs an elastic labour force which can be moved in and out of employment as the market waxes and wanes. This is particularly evident in resource-based boom-or-bust industries such as we have in British Columbia. The welfare state allowed government to be a full adjunct to the development of the corporate economy. The state became the means by which the task of training the population and pulling and pushing labour from one place to another was socialized. The costs are always socialized and the profits are always privatized. That is essentially what the welfare state was all about. Of course, it is true that in addition the welfare state provided minimum conditions of living for the people. Without it things would have been worse. We get caught in a bind.

We have a welfare apparatus which does not solve fundamental economic problems and which, in fact, pacifies the population. The welfare state satisfies people and makes them feel that somehow it is all working. Capitalism appears to be fine when it delivers the goods. In an expanding economy with a welfare state, we could not make the argument that there are fundamental problems. Now we are stuck with a paradox. Changes in technology and very dramatic changes in the organization of the world economic order render much of the labour force, which has been protected by the welfare state, unnecessary. Therefore, in capitalist terms, the welfare state is no longer required. What we are witnessing is the creation of a labour surplus in many industrial countries. As capital is restructured, as it must be within the next decade, the global corporate industrial economy will not need a large labour force, nor will it need to promote the welfare policies that sustain it.

We have to address the restructuring of capital. We have to address the fundamental structuring of the international economy. That is the first economic thing that we have to talk about. That comes prior to attacking or defending legitimation statements. If we get stuck in a position where all we are saying is, "No you're not right–it's not true what you're saying," we are simply accepting the conservatives' premises. We have to address something much more fundamental than ideology.

PLOTKE: It is not clear to me that capital knows what's good for it. It is not clear to me that things fit together quite so neatly between the demands of corporations and the demands of the state. You are right to say that there is going to be a decreasing demand for labour in some sectors of the economy. It is not so clear that demand for qualified labour will decrease throughout the economy. I'm not willing to accept the idea that it is economically rational to destroy the welfare state even from the perspective of capital. It is not in any sense an economically rational strategy. You were verging on suggesting a left wing version of the right's critique of the welfare state. I try to argue that an expanded set of social policies and social spending is economically advantageous.

NEW VOICE: Historically, the welfare state was viewed by pragmatic, well-meaning leftists as a transitional stage between a brutal capitalist system and the egalitarian socialist system we hoped to build. Now, we find ourselves trying to defend something which, quite frankly, I don't think we wanted in the first place. Essentially, the social welfare programs of the 50s and 60s applied the trickle down theory. They took the surplus of a rapidly growing economy and applied it to some of the most obvious and open wounds. If we accept trickle down welfarism, we accept growth as inviolable. We've got to focus on the whole issue of growth. Is growth defined as business raping the Gross National Product? How is it measured? What are the indexes? Evolving an analysis of growth is a challenge for social democrats.

In Europe, "right to work" means the right of workers to productive paid labour. Here, "right to work" is a right wing campaign to smash unions. Canadian accept layoffs as part of their role in the society. They have accepted unemployment and recession as inevitable. In 1983, 40 percent of people polled by the NDP thought that restraint and cutbacks in government services were important, inevitable and necessary. We have done a magnificent job of tying our hands with the ideological tools that could win the battle. We have not attempted to pose any real alternatives. The great American socialist Eugene V. Debbs said, "I would prefer to vote for something I really want and not get it than to vote for something I don't want and get it." The welfare state was something we didn't really want. We got it. It ain't socialism, and we are now in the ridiculous position of defending it. We should be embarrassed by the conservatives who can correctly pin us with every crime of the welfare state. We have lost the image of the egalitarian society. Socialists become the people who marched the kids onto buses, not the people who wanted to eliminate racism. We become the people associated with a strong centralist state. The right has discovered a wonderful tactic which will continue to be successful until we revitalize our imagination and our vision.

NEW VOICE: I appreciated the coherent picture of the conservative critique. Perhaps because Canada is a dependent economy and not an imperial economy, our politicians simply drive straight through and say we can't afford it. If we argue the economic benefits of social programs, then we are probably going to argue for their contribution to aggregate demand and their possible assistance to social adjustment in relation to changing technology and the changing international economy. Those economic arguments aren't winning the day. I perceive a very powerful right wing populist dynamic. There is something about that populist thrust that appeals, perhaps, to a fundamental conservative concern for neighbourhoods and communities and to perceptions of the state and the delivery of social programs. Public sector unions are always open to the accusation that they are defending their jobs. We cannot win the battle for social programs on the ground of defending people who are perceived as having a great deal of job security.

PLOTKE: The situation in the United States is rather preposterous. There is an overwhelming critique of welfare statism without quite having a welfare state. It's not as though we have national health insurance in the United States. Most people perceive the state as inefficient and highly bureaucratic in its delivery of services, and insensitive to differences and community forms. In the United States if you want to say something is inefficient, you say it is like the post office. If something is authoritarian, it is like the army. If something is slow, it is like the Department of Motor Vehicles. People think that the market is efficient if impersonal, that communities are personal if not necessarily efficient, and that the state is impersonal and inefficient, combining the worst features of both.

I agree that when we got the welfare state we didn't get what we wanted. We did not get democratic forms of state or community administration, construction or involvement. How do you change forms of implementation and construction of social policy measures so that they are seen as democratic and popular?

The debate as to whether current changes in technology and in the world economy are mainly deskilling work or are having more mixed effects is significant. If you think the results will be to deskill and dequalify labour, then my argument will seem purely and simply wrong. However, I think technological change will have much more mixed and complicated effects. We will have to make a human capital argument to justify expansion of social policy. The measures necessary to cope with technological changes are not going to be borne by private firms. An expanded social policy network is going to be one of the few ways to protect workers from displacement. In the Bay Area, there used to be big automobile production facilities which are all closed. Nobody is responsible for retraining auto workers. The United Auto Workers [UAW] can't do it. The automobile companies don't want to do it. It is unacceptable that no effort is made to retrain the thousands of skilled people displaced from the automobile industry, that their skills are abandoned rather than adapted to the new sectors. That's a social policy area that is economically effective. You can make a social policy argument about human capital. Accepting deskilling implicitly accepts that displaced workers should work in McDonalds.

NEW VOICE: I must reinforce the statement that conservative arguments about social policy cannot be addressed by heaping condemnation on criticism of the size of the public sector, the size of transfer payments and various other welfare policies. It is very important to distinguish two arguments. There is the ultraconservative argument which wants to disband the public sector and dismantle the welfare state, and the more libertarian conservative argument that just wants to push things back. We, as social democrats, have been very guilty of not distinguishing between the two. To take a very humble local example, a poll taking during the last provincial election (May, 1983) indicated that fully three quarters of the population wanted some kind of restraint policy. Exactly what the electorate thought they wanted, God only knows. But we were incapable of addressing the issues. What should be the size of the public sector? What should be our responsibility *qua* employer vis a vis public sector unions? What kind of wage and salary policies should we pursue? We were incapable of addressing those issues because of conflicts inherent in our simultaneous alliance with labour. It is not sinful for us to address the issue of what should be the size of the state.

The human capital argument should be taken very seriously. One of the strengths we have left is an idea that is very strong among the population. There is popular support for the idea that unemployment is fundamentally a disaster because you lose skills and you lose self-respect. The electorate recognizes the many external costs of unemployment.

In the 1930s we weren't ashamed to direct public policy towards direct job creation. The left does not emphasize nearly enough that part of social policy must be job creation for those with low human capital and low skills. I think we should be prepared, as many social democratic parties in Europe are, to argue explicitly for wage subsidies at the lower end.

One of the nice distinctions to be made between the United States and Canada is that, unlike the U.S., Canada still has provincial and municipal levels of government with a degree of competence and an ability to administer. Far worse in the United States than in Canada is the sense that only the Federal government is capable of generating a protective safety net for the people at the bottom. The sense that local governments are the bastions of racism and reaction is not a syndrome within Canada. It is very important that we don't slip into this dilemma. For example, Monique Begin, the former federal Health Minister championed herself as the sole bastion of the medicare system against all those god forsaken provincial governments who would transfer all the money from welfare programs and pave over their provinces if only she would let them. That historically is not true. Medicare began in this country in the province of Saskatchewan under a democratic socialist government. It is very important that we address the issue of preserving local administrative units to administer social programs.

NEW VOICE: We have to distinguish between long-term and short-term goals. We have to have some concept of the way things could be different from the way they are. Rather than reinforcing the way things are by criticizing them, we've got to have a concept of something different. Therefore, it is extremely important that we examine our definitions.

What do we mean by growth? Do we mean large department stores with thousands upon thousands of new garments which are seasonally obsolete when fashion changes? Do we mean seventeen kinds of deodorant? Is that really growth or is that simply serving the interests of the corporate structure?

We need a new definition of wealth. There has never been any real redistribution of wealth in this country or any other capitalist country. We redistribute some of the income, but not in a way that changes the relationship between the rich and the poor. In fact the poor are getting marginally poorer and the rich are getting richer. We need to get away from the idea of acceptable levels of poverty. The utility to capitalism of an elastic labour force is important. When a signficant segment of the labour force becomes redundant it may not be rational for corporate capitalism to say it will not continue to serve those people, but I don't think we can rely on capitalism to be rational. It has never been rational in the past, why should it be rational in the future? The rationality of a society which spends over a million dollars a minute on armaments surely has to be called into question.

We need a new definition of economics. We keep talking about the economy as if it were reified, fixed, permanent, universal. We confuse economics with commerce. An International Labour Organization [ILO] study from 1980 shows that women do two thirds of the world's work hours, produce 44 percent of the world's food supply, receive 10 percent of the world's wages and own 1 percent real property. Does that suggest a rational definition of economy?

We need a new definition of work. Perhaps we also need a new definition of family. We have concentrated urban societies which are hooked into fossil fuels and are ruled by corporate elites. We pretend that we still have the Dickensian family with Momma and Poppa and three children at the fireside knitting bedsocks for Christmas. That family doesn't exist any more. In the short term, we have got to find ways of preventing the erosion of the relatively minimal level of social policy that we have, and in the long term we've got to examine what a redistribution of wealth would really mean and take into account the fact that we are moving into a post-industrial state.

NEW VOICE: As a Canadian I have trouble with across-the-border comparisons with the United States. Canada's link

with the British tradition is much stronger. Americans generally view the economy almost as a given, while in Canada the
concept is not so rigid. There is a tradition of an alternate
vision because Canada is not an economic country. Our
vision is somewhat unique. It is a rather strange mix which is
not economic in a lot of ways. We have lived with that and, in
some ways, we like it. We do not have a racial question tied to
poverty to the degree that the United States does. There are
analogies with our native people and their problems are
acute and embarrassing. However, because of their numbers,
their needs do not become a problem that affects universal
social policy. Certainly, one can agree that the question of
linking the family, community and neighbourhood is important in terms of the left's vision of society.

Canada has a different tradition in the public sector. We
have been more willing to intervene massively in the economy.
Governments have undertaken projects that the private sector would never touch–national railways, airlines, potash
plants, the medicare system. In order to provide services to
the frontier that private enterprise would not, and perhaps
could not, deliver, government has done incredible, un-
economic things. There is a different tradition here.

There is also a different tradition in terms of regionalism.
The regions of Canada are strong. They have a land resource
rent base that is phenomenal. They have independent revenue potential because of very different ownership patterns. In
British Columbia, the Crown owns 95 percent of the land.
Imagine what that would be in California. This is a legal reality
in Canada, not a philosophical socialist debate.

The tradition of the left in this country is one of an
alternative economic vision, which frequently has been tied
to ethical rather than economic considerations. That is the
critical question we should be addressing. What is this
alternative economic vision? It is not just social welfare
decorating the edges of the existing capitalist system.

PLOTKE: I hope that the differences you perceive between
Canadian and American political culture persist. They all
seem to be to your advantage. I remain, however, slightly

sceptical. The differences between Canada and the United States that you have pointed out are even sharper between Britain and the United States. Historically, Britain's socialist and labour traditions are larger and stronger than those in Canada or the U.S. Today Britain has a much more virulently free market, monetarist, right wing populist government than that of Ronald Reagan. I hope that those differences to which you allude can preserve Canada from a Reaganite future. In the current situation, the boundaries between economic and social policies that were accepted on the right and the left in the United States in the 40s, 50s and 60s, are breaking down. It is now possible to interrelate economic and social policies in new ways. This situation for the left in the United States is not hopeless. It is now possible to make a social policy argument that cuts into and refutes the idea of an autonomous economy which simply has to be respected. It is now possible to argue that the economy is another human institution which is actually constructed.

POWER TO THE END USER*

Margaret Lowe Benston
Department of Computing Science
and
Women's Studies Program
Simon Fraser University
Burnaby, B.C.

THE MYSTIQUE WHICH SURROUNDS TECHNOLOGY and expertise is problematic and pervasive in our culture. We labour under the delusion that you have to be an expert to understand technology. Ordinary people do not get a chance to talk about it. My training is as a chemist. I have no formal credentials for either of the jobs that I do, a personal affirmation of my belief that non-experts should run the society.

Technology is not neutral. Production technology embodies capitalist social relations in its structure. Science and

* The article "Power to the End User" is an edited transcription of Prof. Benston's presentation to a discussion group which focused on The Economy. Her paper "A New Technology" differs substantially from this article and is recommended to readers interested in technological change. The paper is available from the Boag Foundation.

capitalist society are so intertwined that it is impossible to separate them. There isn't a technology and a society. This is a technological society based on chemical, mechanical and, increasingly, electronic technologies. Capitalism and technology are two aspects of the same phenomenon. They go together.

Technology arises from specific social contexts and has to be understood in terms of specific social contexts. This thesis is well developed by Harry Braverman in his book *Labor and Monopoly Capital*. Historically, the role of technology in the workplace has been quite consistent. New technologies are introduced to increase productivity and to increase control over the work force by increasing management's ability to manipulate and intervene in the labour process. The dominant mode of mass production for the last 50 years has been Taylorism. Taylor believed fanatically that workers, given half a chance, would "soldier" on the job, tell lies to management and probably sit around playing pinochle. Management's job was to extract every second of work out of the time that they bought as labour power.

Technology is intended to enhance management's job. The most logical combination, in the area of mechanical automation, is the assembly line. Assembly lines are antithetical to social democratic organization. We cannot take over the line and turn it into a socialist tool. Those kinds of technologies have to be dismantled and replaced. This is not to say that components of the system are not relatively neutral, but once assembled they enforce a specific relationship.

Electronic technology comes out of the same process. The idea that it is inevitable and that workers must adjust to it must be fought. This technology may be inevitable under capitalism. However, as socialists we need to analyse it, expose it and resist it, not adapt to it or welcome it. Pollution, war and waste are also inevitable under capitalism!

The new technology is part of a historical continuity. Computers are machines like any other, introduced for historically familiar purposes–to make profits for business. But quantitatively, and perhaps qualitatively, it is unlike other technologies. It is a new phenomenon because of the enormous productivity gains it makes possible. Developments in the capacity and cost of computer power demonstrate an inverse relationship. Capacity is increasing and cost is decreasing and these changes are occurring incredibly rapidly. It has been estimated that if the aeronautics industry had developed at the same rate as the computing industry, a Boeing 747 could circle the globe in 5 minutes burning $2.00 worth of fuel. Electronic technology is cheap. The cost of computing power and memory has dropped by a factor of 1,000 over the past fifteen years.

Both cheap and effective, it is being introduced right across the workplace. In the past, technological change has been limited to one area of the economy at a time. The process of decreasing costs and increasing power will continue for the next ten years at least. The industry predicts that costs will continue to drop over the next fifteen to twenty years. As costs drop, we will see the social effects magnified. Any strategy that socialists develop has to take into account that we are not looking at a finished technology. Electronic technology is not in place, nor is its ultimate capacity predictable.

The new technology affects more than just the means of production. Among other things, it will redefine what we mean by productivity. Productivity is not a neutral world. Prior to the mechanization of agriculture, one kind of productivity was defined as farm output measured against farm horses. Using this definition, for the first ten years after the introduction of tractors, the productivity of horses rises as the number of horses declines. The productivity of the last horse is pretty much infinite. The old definition of productivity, which is strictly output per number of workers, will become less and less meaningful in terms of the potential of the new kinds of machines. It becomes a political issue.

Since the Second World War, and until recently, the economies of western industrialized countries have been characterized by economic growth and expanding employment opportunities. This had implications for unions and for the structure of the labour force. During that period, there was an accommodation by unions with capital. The Keynesian bargain was that capital would guarantee full employment and rising wages. The union leadership would deliver a depoliticized membership which did not question management rights or want to talk about the work process but which would settle for economic gains. This bargain was made possible by an expanding economy and growth in employment. Women, in their historical function as a reserve army of labour, were called up. Women, particularly married women, entered the active wage-labour force. Today, significant numbers of households in Canada depend on two incomes to maintain an ordinary style of living. The majority of married women who work are living with men whose incomes are less than average.

The long postwar expansionary period is highly unusual in the history of capitalism. The tendency of domestic and world markets to expand and for the labour force to be stable has not been smooth or automatic. The First World War increased employment needs through stimulation of demand, during and immediately after the war. By 1918, there was a major slump with high unemployment followed by fewer than ten years of prosperity, followed by the Depression, followed by the Second World War. World War II shattered the productive capacities of the industrialized countries and consequently stimulated demand, so much so that any economic policy probably would have worked. Postwar demand, coupled with social policies explicitly founded on deficit spending, stimulated the economy and the growth in employment. However, a careful study of job creation shows that almost all of the new jobs were created in the public sector, in education, public service and, in the United States, in the military. Capitalism cannot make the case that the last 30 years have been normal times and that we should judge our response and our analysis of the effects of technology on that basis, nor can the private sector claim to be the engine of job creation. In fact, stagnation, underemployment and unemployment are endemic to capitalism. Our strategies should reflect that fact.

Scenario: The Last Two Canadian Workers

Cast: Two workers
One is Male. One is Female.
(We have won the fight for sex equality!)

Set: A very large industrial plant.
Universal Ubiquitous Acme Productions,
Canadian Branch

Action: The Male Worker: Starts the Machine
The Female Worker: Shuts it Down.

Result: Goods and Services for the Canadian
Population

If it is a capitalist system, under welfare state logic, they are each paid something like $999,999,999 a year and taxed $999,979,999 a year, which is then given in welfare to the Canadian population. This is clearly absurd. But if we are up to 20 percent real unemployment, if full employment is defined as 30 percent unemployment, when does it stop being normal and become absurd in terms of the relationship of unemployment to the productive capacity?

The redistribution of work has to be looked at. Capitalist economic logic does not provide a solution to the *reductio ad absurdum* scenario. The mechanism for the distribution of production is through the wage relation. That is how social credits are obtained to buy goods and to distribute goods. When the wage relation is distorted, through increased technological productivity with concomitant increases in unemployment, the distribution system is also distorted. In the short run, the logic of the system allows more goods to be produced than can be distributed. In the long run, workers absorb the costs of disequilibrium in the system.

We are not dependent on automation for prosperity. We have had an industrial base that can produce enough for everybody since at least the 1930s. Industrialists have been revamping, retooling, renovating on the basis of profit and not on the basis of human need. The ability to produce is unrelated to human needs and to the ability to distribute.

She quits, and goes back home to her real work

We are looking at developments which are the consequence of trying to maintain an economic system in the face of forces that appear to be pushing it over a cliff. These developments will affect men and women in different ways. Women have historically been a reserve army of labour. Today they are less in reserve. Just over half of the women in Canada view themselves as part of the wage-labour force. Forty percent of the labour force is now female. Women's work is ghettoized, restricted to well-defined areas which most likely will contract as a result of automation. The increasing implementation of office automation systems will continue. Historically, offices have been under-capitalized relative to manufacturing sectors. As the new technology gets cheaper and cheaper, the amount of capital required for potentially very large productivity gains is relatively small. It seems inevitable that the number of jobs in the clerical sector will decline. The creation of adequate jobs to replace those lost to automation in offices is highly unlikely.

The technology itself does not create a lot of new jobs. We are not going to be a nation of computer programmers. Programming is being automated. Chip production is being automated. Electronic maintenance and repair is being automated. Because of high unemployment and sex segregation in the wage-labour force, men will get first crack at whatever new jobs are created. The present distribution of power in the society makes it unlikely that women will have equal access. Women's jobs will contract and the unemployment rate will rise, unless a number of people choose to withdraw "voluntarily" from the labour market. The prime candidates for voluntary withdrawal are women. This is, historically, how a reserve army of labour works. When the demand for labour falls, it is convenient if a significant section of the work force can simply vanish back into the home, maintaining the current inequitable power distribution between men and women.

Some of the most compelling evidence for the change in attitudes toward women in the work force is the success of

the new right in the United States. The new right has taken on
women's roles as an area of political struggle. They have taken
a very conservative view of women's roles. There are also
indications of changing attitudes in popular culture. The hit
movie *Mr. Mom* presents a not so subliminal message.

> Mr. Mom works in the home
> and learns to do it very well
> of course he can do it
> she's an executive
> he's lost his job
> he gets his job back
> she gets sexually harassed by her boss
>   and can't take it
> poor dear
>   so SHE QUITS
>   and GOES BACK HOME
>   to her REAL WORK

The left is not addressing the right wing attack on women.
Feminism is not seen as an integral part of the socialist
program. Ten years ago I was trying to convince people that
we should not have to say we were socialist feminists because
a proper understanding of socialism would take for granted
that you were also a feminist. Any real socialist vision has to
include a society where women are not disadvantaged. After
ten years we still have to maintain that we are socialist
feminists. It is still hard to convince male socialists that we are
real socialists if we insist on being feminists.

The results of technological change will enhance the
ideological and actual discrimination against women in the
very near future. Cuts in social spending mean that many
services, now provided in the public domain, will be thrown
back on private individuals. Who is going to be available to
provide private social services? It would be handy if it were
women. A conservative ideology reinforces the notion that
women ought to be in the home, nurturing their children,
and doing community service.

The role of women in the workplace will likely be exploited by capital to the detriment of the male work force. During the period of transition to complete automation, women will continue to be employed in low paying, non-unionized, assembly line sectors. Women, historically, have been seen as a useful part of the wage-labour force because they are docile. They aren't highly unionized. They are more patient with horrible working conditions. Women's socialization conditions them to believe that it is inappropriate for them to be active trade unionists. Social democratic parties and labour unions have to direct energy toward unionizing women. The people who are trying to unionize office workers in the United States have a slogan: "The office of the future is the factory of the past."

There are many signals that women will be used to make high technology succeed for capitalism. Clearly, problems with this strategy should be explored and exploited by democratic socialists. Withdrawal of women from the labour force will result in a drop in family standards of living. Unemployed women, as non-wage workers, substituting their labour in the home, will affect the demand for goods and services. The women's movement will be problematic for this capitalist strategy. So, we hope, will the socialist movement. The protection of the very limited gains that women have made over the last 40 years must be a priority on any socialist program. The threat to women follows directly from the new technology. The threat to unions is every bit as great as the threat to women. The new technology will be used as a weapon to break the power of unions. The unions are still playing by the Keynesian rules of the ball game, but the bosses have changed the rules. They are moving work out of unionized sectors. Union membership is declining. The ability to resist the new technology has not even begun to be developed. The current situation cries out for attention. How can unions become more political? How can people in the workplace begin discussions of the work process and industrial democracy? The problems that the new technology creates for workers, particularly the very negative effects for women, must be high on the socialist agenda.

DISCUSSION

NEW VOICE: On its October 20, 1983, edition, CBC's *Journal* did a special report on the garment industry in Montreal. Some of the conditions normally associated with Third World countries are happening here in Canada. The garment industry is trying to break up unions by farming work out to contractors who employ women working in their homes. This is the worst kind of exploitative labour. Control is taken from organized workers and the work is given to women who are isolated and who have absolutely no protection against the contractor.

NEW VOICE: That is not only happening in the garment industry, it is happening to farm workers and transportation workers. They don't hire people now, they hire a contractor who provides them with workers. Many contractors have no knowledge of, or respect for, labour laws.

BENSTON: Part-time work is the fastest growing category of jobs. Admittedly, these figures never extrapolate exactly, but if the present trends continue, by the year 2000 half of all the jobs in Canada will be part-time.

NEW VOICE: The relationship between unemployment and the new high technology is very complex. I have reservations about concluding that high unemployment is inevitable under the new technology. I would be more comfortable with the conclusion that high unemployment is inevitable under the current structure of the economic order. New technology may be inevitable, but unemployment is not inevitable. Unemployment is a problem that can be addressed. Lack of clear understanding and specific policies to counter the complex problem of contemporary unemployment are failures of social democratic movements. There is a tendency to blame high unemployment on something objective. We do not look at the relationships of production but rather for scapegoats like high technology which are objective in the sense that they are material and removed from the structural relationship.

BENSTON: I agree. My conclusion is, I think, justified in that if high technology continues to be put in place, with no change in the industrial or political policies, high unemployment is as inevitable as high technology. However, you are right about not losing sight of the underlying structure. The argument about whether unemployment is structural to capitalism has been going on for years. I am not a trained economist, but my intuition, supported by everything I've read so far, indicates that stagnation and underemployment are the inevitable results of "normal" capitalist economic logic. They can slow it down and fiddle with it in various ways but the curve is downhill with fluctuations on the curve.

Let's forget about any real strategic considerations for a moment and simplify. There must be some more equitable way of dividing up what work there is and providing mechanisms for distributing what's produced. We clearly have enough people to produce what is needed and we clearly have an industrial base. Indeed, our industrial base is so overbuilt for our needs right now that it is ludicrous.

NEW VOICE: And there clearly are enough needs.

NEW VOICE: In the last five or six decades there has been a growing number of people who work servicing high technology workers. If you concentrate your argument on redistributing work, you defuse the argument that the objective should be redistributing income.

BENSTON: You have to argue for the right of people who want work to have it, as well as for income redistribution. There is evidence that people want work. The fight for a reduced work week has to go with maintaining wages.

NEW VOICE: The federal government has made a veiled attempt to redefine the employment/unemployment rate relative to the marked increase in the participation rate over the last 30 years. They are starting to argue that, if we look at the participation rate of ten years ago, what looks like 12 percent unemployment is actually 2 percent unemployment. Therefore, we are working in a full employment economy. This ignores substantial empirical evidence from industrial economies which have managed to sustain 3 percent unemployment in a non-inflationary manner. This gets us to Incomes Policy.

Historically, there have been adaptations to tremendous changes in the manner of production, distribution and exchange. We are going through a profound structural change which gravely affects women workers and we have to do something about that in the immediate context. I would argue that it should be through redistributive policies.

The consequence of not adapting to new technologies will be to cut real wage rates in half. If we do not increase productivity, wage rates will have to go down. If we deliberately over-staff or maintain jobs which are not commercially viable in an economic market, something has to give and that something is usually the wage rate. We have to adapt to the new technology. We cannot take an anti-technology or an anti-change stand.

BENSTON: What do you mean "adapt" to the new technology?

NEW VOICE: Microtechnology and computer technology is here with us and it is not going away.

BENSTON: Capitalism is here with us and it is not going away. They are the same thing right now.

NEW VOICE: Capitalism and computer technology are not the same thing.

BENSTON: The computer technology we have now is capitalist technology.

NEW VOICE: It is not the technology, it is how you use it.

BENSTON: No, it is not. It is an entire system. It is how you build it. An assembly line is a specific kind of technology. It is an anti-human technology.

NEW VOICE: We cannot simply ignore high technology.

BENSTON: I did not say we should ignore it. I am not in total disagreement with you. I am positing negative strategies. People say, it's here to stay, we can't avoid it, we must adapt to it. That's the current jargon. We have to examine that very carefully. If adapting means that we have to accept capitalist logic, capitalist rules, degradation of the workplace, rising unemployment, then I say that as socialists we don't. We have to argue that current methods of implementing computer technology are anti-human. We should pose alternatives that encourage workers to be critical. People who are displaced by machines know those machines are bad for them. If we tell workers they have to adapt, we are cutting our own throats because we are telling lies that contradict people's experience in the workplace. We have to have a program which acknowledges what's actually happening to workers.

NEW VOICE: I have problems with the distinction between capitalist and socialist technology. Could you describe "socialist technology"?

BENSTON: O.K. Is it socialism if we take over the banks and computer systems and simply use the software and the hardware they've got? Do we have to develop our own financial systems with different patterns of centralization and decentralization and a hardware and software configuration to support the kind of decentralization we want? I'd say yes. We want a different kind of system. If we want a decentralized government where decision-making power goes back to people at the local level, then we have to have computer systems that are decentralized. Current systems are highly bureaucratized and incorporate and solidify the logic of the agencies. They are simply not suitable to a decentralized system.

A brief technical lesson. A star network is a basic hardware configuration with a central large computer and a whole bunch of passive terminals hanging off of it. The programs are written and implemented at the centre. All the messages between terminals go through the central computer. That's one model for electronic mail. It opens up lovely possibilities for surveillance. Or you can have a decentralized network where computing power resides in the terminal. There is no central computer at all. There are local programs. Local people put in the information and share it locally. Control and monitoring cannot be imposed through a central program because there isn't one. Those are two completely different kinds of technology all built with terminals and chips and software.

NEW VOICE: I am leery about the idea that technology is going to result, sooner or later, in stopping the growth of employment. That assumes that there is, in some sense, a limit to how much we can consume and how much we are going to produce in our society as we increase productivity because of new technology. This implies a drastic decline in the amount of work. I am not yet confident of that. The participation rates listed in *The Annual Economic Review* (1982) indicate that Canada, in the last decade, had the second fastest growing labour force. There was not much decline in the average hours worked overall. We should not think of technology as drastically reducing work. A reduced work week with the same rate of pay, in other terms, says redistribution. Less work for the same wage comes out of somebody's hide; it implies a poverty income in one way shape or form. There is some potential for that, but only some.

BENSTON: Traditional analytical tools may be outstripped by the magnitude of the effects of high technology. There are many studies that make a strong case for the anti-employment effects of technology. We must not forget that chip-based business systems are roughly five years old. The technology is not in place. We have not seen the final effect. They are still only potential, but when you look at the systems which are in place and working, the trend is clear.

High technology can deliver enormous productivity gains. Historically, some of the gains from technological change have been passed back to workers, when they bargain for them, in the form of a shorter work week, which means more jobs for everybody, or higher wages, or both. The demand for a shorter work week without a reduction in wages, merely states the case for passing some of the new gains back to workers. The work week has gone from something like 60 hours to 37.5 over the last 40 years.

NEW VOICE: People have been predicting massive technological unemployment for a hundred years or more. Everybody always thinks that the latest technology is unique, impressive and threatening. Usually that is just not the case. The right wing is gaining the votes of the public. If we adopt an anti-technological stance, that is bound to continue. Resisting the new technology and sharing existing work is an extremely negative approach which guarantees lower living standards while people in other countries are likely to be experiencing higher living standards. As a political program, that's a recipe for disaster. Japan, Sweden, Norway and Austria have managed to maintain extremely low unemployment rates. Those are mainly countries that have kept inflation under control through policies other than deliberate monetarist creation of unemployment. The challenge lies in that direction. The main threat to employment comes through monetarism rather than technology.

NEW VOICE: There is an important difference between opposing a new technology and opposing the way it is organized and imposed. Historically, the effect of the introduction of technology has been to eliminate the worker, to remove the unreliable factor which can go on strike. A computer operated machine, or any machine, works without the threat of job action. The current definition of work and full employment reflects and creates problems, one of which is: how are the rewards to the individual to be determined? So far, that determination has been a measure of the value of individual productivity to the capitalist, not to the society. We pay a hell of a lot of money to a fellow who can shove a football along the ground, whereas we ignore the people who are delivering social services. They are underpaid and undermanned. We also ignore the people who bring up our children. How do we decide? How we answer that question will, to a large extent, determine how we deal with the problems of technology.

NEW VOICE: We cannot disregard the benefits of technological change. Today technologies are in place which elevate rather than degrade work. Technology has eliminated all kinds of miserable, back breaking work on production lines. Workers always oppose change until they receive some guarantee of employment.

BENSTON: There are uses, particularly of small computers, which increase productivity and expand control, creativity and enjoyment. The positive side needs to be emphasized. Small, decentralized systems are useful. But we must be very careful not to swallow the computer industry's advertising campaign wholesale. If we can win something in return for dirty boring jobs being automated, we should do that, but we need a trade off because jobs are being given up. We need social clout. Individual unions have been fighting for the trade off, but it is clearly not winnable at the level of an individual workplace. The postal workers have got the best tech change clauses in Canada and they think they're losing about a thousand jobs a year to technological change. Unions have to take on technological change as a wider political issue, but they have to take it on together, not union by union. However, even unions acting together are not strong enough. Only 20 percent of the work force, and going down hill all the time, is organized.

We have to insist that these machines be introduced for human good. If social democrats embrace this technology uncritically, we will find a lot of workers who know better and who will reject it and us.

NEW VOICE: I am upset by the people in this room who are suggesting that we adapt to this technology. The industrial implementation of high technology means that we are going to lose jobs. I'll give you a classic example from the brewery industry. I work there and I know the numbers. It takes 35 people to produce beer on a bottle line. It takes seven people to produce beer on an automated can line. We're fighting like hell to stop the cans. Don't buy canned beer. It is reducing our work force. It has cut Labatt's workers by one third. Don't tell me that we have to adapt to it, goddam it. We're not going to adapt to it. We're going to fight it. We're going to sabotage it. We're going to do everything we can. We're going to stop the line.

NEW VOICE: If you drink canned beer, drink more!

NEW VOICE: On an immediate, individual level, policies have to be in place before change is allowed to occur. I don't like my job. It's boring, it's repetitive, it's monotonous, it's dirty. But don't anybody suggest to me that you're going to take my job away, because I'm not going to have another one to replace it. I want to keep my boring, monotonous, dirty job. I am anti-technology if it means I don't have a job.

NEW VOICE: I work in an area where technology has increased my capabilities tremendously. I'm an investment broker. The computer system gives me rapid access to a lot of information which helps me serve my clients. Certainly there are fewer and fewer blue collar workers because of technology, but we have had an increase in the service sector. I'm not convinced that with the decreasing number of people in the beer line there won't be more jobs created in other sectors that will pick up the slack. Nobody knows what the future looks like. When I was in high school I wrote a paper about a Westinghouse light bulb plant which reduced its work force from 300 to seven—five guys to sweep the floors and two guys to watch the gauges. That didn't mean we had massive unemployment in the 60s.

BENSTON: We had an expanding economy for very unusual reasons.

NEW VOICE: If you don't have an expanding economy and you attempt to maintain the number of people on a line you are going to have a decreasing pie. There is no other way of cutting it. You have to have an increasing pie so you can take care of everybody. If the same wages are gained for less work, you've got to have a growing economy.

BENSTON: You're giving the capitalist line. You're telling me how capitalism works. I know how capitalism works.

NEW VOICE: I am not talking about capitalism. I'm talking about the economic base which says that you can only divide the pie so many times. Whether you give the big slice to the workers or to the profit sector is immaterial. The pie is only so big.

NEW VOICE: Lenin defined socialism as electricity plus Soviets.

QUALITY OF WORK
The Doors of Perception*

David Schreck
Secretary
Pacific Group for Policy Alternatives
Vancouver, B.C.

I WAS PART OF GROUP WHICH ARGUED before the MacDonald Commission [a federal Royal Commission on the economy] for two objectives, essentially plagiarized from the Canadian Catholic Bishops' statement. The first included recognition of the priority of labour and recognition of the importance of social programs. We need policies which recognize the importance of social programs to defuse the right wing attack. The second recommendation was for straightforward Keynesian expansionism and stimulus, which, combined with employment planning, reject the concept of market supremacy in which individuals bear the responsibility for transition. A fundamental structural problem in our economy is that individuals rather than society bear the cost of change.

*The article "Quality of Work: The Doors of Perception" is an edited transcription of Mr. Schreck's presentation to a discussion group which focused on The Economy.

116

Technologies which can increase productivity imply a moral responsibility to improve output. We rejected arguments which emphasize coping with change rather than using it to our advantage. Therefore, we rejected decreasing the work week or increasing leisure time either voluntarily or involuntarily. We argued that if we *can* produce more, we have a *responsibility* to produce more as long as there are people inadequately fed and housed. Our problem is not the lack of ability to increase production. The problem lies with a social structure that exploits increased productivity for the greater profit of a few while a larger number of individuals bear the cost of that transition. Along with a traditional attack on monetarism, we made reference to the Japanese model with regard to layoffs and retraining.

The problems which arise from stimulating an individual economy do not have to do with leakage through the money market; they have to do with normal import leakage. Economies are becoming more interdependent. Just over 30 percent of the Canadian Gross National Product [GNP] is exported and a corresponding amount imported. As we increase productive capacity we import more. That form of leakage is what is draining off the stimulus. It does not have to do with the operation of the money market. The money market facilitates trade, it does not cause the problem. Rather than opposing barriers to trade, we should argue that we have a responsibility to see the Third World develop. Moreover, we should see it as an opportunity to develop more markets. It is to our benefit to have living standards increased throughout the world. If we feel threatened by Third World competition, we are really operating contrary to our own objectives.

DISCUSSION

NEW VOICE: I would like to make a small point about the extent to which any one country can have Keynesian expansion in view of the global nature of the problem. Certainly it is the conventional wisdom that France fell, partly because of the increase of imports, but also because the international money market cut the French franc. It is not often realized that, in relation to GNP, the amount of fiscal expansion in the Reagan administration was larger than Mitterand's expansion. In other words, Reagan was more Keynesian than Mitterand. During this period the U.S. dollar soared and the French franc dropped like a stone. It depends not so much on the extent of the expansion as on the political expression of the government doing the expanding. The international money markets are conservative and will have more confidence in right wing expansion than in left wing expansion.

NEW VOICE: People percolating around the edges of social democratic parties are dabbling with the idea of changing the ownership structure of the means of production. In addition to the present owners of the means of production, the trade union movement will be deeply affected by any changes in that area. The trade union movement has become a reflection of the present form of ownership. If you change the means of production, it follows that you will have a major effect on trade unions. We are seeing some re-examination of the relationship between Canadian social democratic parties and the trade union movement. I feel acutely any suggestion that the proper response is to make that relationship more distant. Social democratic parties are coming forward with suggestions that are going to fundamentally affect the trade union movement. There are some within the trade union movement who view that as a frontal assault.

When a social democratic party was in power in the province of Saskatchewan, I was one of a group of people from government and the trade union movement whose mandate was simply to think and talk about management structures and employee relationships within Crown corporations. The group met for two or three months and was just starting to gel when the Saskatchewan Federation of Labour [SFL] held its annual convention. The labour representative on the committee decided to make a presentation to the SFL. This resulted in an interesting alliance between the extreme left and extreme right of the SFL and a resounding rejection of the tentative, timorous efforts to examine, let alone change, management structures. To an extent, that can be explained because we are all afraid of change. But to a greater extent, it represented a knee-jerk reaction by the trade union movement. What we were talking about would significantly affect the trade union movement's role and raised threatening and unanswered questions. Who does the union relate to? How does it relate to members and employees? To what extent do employees bypass the trade union structure if, in fact, they are given some form of control over the management of the enterprise that they work in? Those things raise the hackles of the trade union movement. The committee died a natural death.

There are people here from the trade union movement and people active within social democratic parties. They are all ideologues of the left. If anyone is going to foment and stimulate a change in the structure of the workplace and the relationship of people in the workplace to the work they do, it is going to be us. Social democratic parties are the only political parties with the capacity to sit down with the trade union movement as friends. We must garner their support, if not accept their leadership, in changing what happens at the point of production. The association with the trade union movement should not be an impediment to the changes that social democratic parties must suggest. Rather, it should be a lever which offers the best chance for changing the relationship of employees to the enterprise.

NEW VOICE: Over the last four years I have done research under the guidance of the Canadian Labour Congress [CLC] and the British Columbia Federation of Labour [BCFL]. In November, 1983, we will present the BCFL with a critique and background paper on Quality of Work which discusses employee involvement and humanization of work. We deal with present theory and describe who is involved and why it is used and approved of by management, how it improves productivity and employment relations, and decreases walk-outs and strikes. I don't know what's going to happen when it gets to the floor. We are not presenting a very positive point of view so we may not get a response like that of the SFL.

However, it is going to leave the unions who are involved in those programs in a very difficult position.

I am appalled by trade unionists and socialists who look to Japan as a positive model of industrial relations, as a country which has supposedly dealt with its population in a better way. It hasn't. There is no such thing as lifetime employment. There are no pension plans. A quarter of the male work force in large corporations work for the company until they reach 55. After 55 they work for a subcontracting firm at a third of their regular wages doing exactly the same job or are supported by their families. Women are forced out of the work force when they marry.

SCHRECK: Japan is undoubtedly an inappropriate model to use in this forum. It was mentioned in the brief to the MacDonald Commission with reference to opposing layoffs. Our current economy accepts layoffs as a method of operation. Layoffs shift the cost of transition onto the individual. Whether we require large corporations to bear part of the cost or whether we bear it collectively, we have to prohibit layoffs as a mechanism of transition. We must insist that there be assignment to other jobs or retraining. The sectors of the Canadian economy that have relatively low first impact leakage indicate where we should apply stimulus. They are largely public sector service-oriented projects like public education and the arts. These are labour intensive sectors which employ almost entirely Canadian labour as opposed to megaprojects which use imported capital, labour, technology and equipment.

NEW VOICE: At best, quality of work life experiments have been an effort to co-opt employees and unions, and at worst they are a form of employee subversion. There is an interest-ing dimension that comes from within management that one should not overlook. The management ethic is not simply a philosophy but a religion. Its dogma insists that it be hierarchical, that there be a corporate structure with a flow sheet showing where you are. Management may feel that, through quality of work experiments, they are co-opting workers and reinforcing the position of superiority/inferiority that is at the heart of management structures. They do not realize that they are allowing a management heresy to develop. The quality of work life movement is an interesting venture in the sense that it may do something to break down the belief that management is, of its essence, "I order, you obey." This tenet permeates all management structures and forms the foundation of hierarchical management organizations.

NEW VOICE: Our present form of society includes class attitudes in management. Breaking down those attitudes is a formidable task which must be approached on a number of fronts, including collective bargaining. Can collective bargaining be used as a tool to achieve change? The example from Saskatchewan came through as a worthy attempt, but still somewhat imposed from above, which may be why there was a very defensive reaction. The trade union movement's skepticism is well founded. We must move carefully as we explore these things politically. People must be persuaded– not coerced. The trade union movement must not only be involved, it must support any changes in the economic structure such as Incomes Policy and democratization of the workplace, if such policy ventures are to be politically successful.

NEW VOICE: The lack of democracy in the workplace is compounded by workers' acceptance of authoritarian structures. It is very rare, in my experience, to find a workplace where the workers say, "Hell, we should be running this." Quality of work experiments are sometimes touted as participatory democracy. What it really comes down to is letting workers vote on what colour to paint the door so they will feel happy as they push through it. We are trying to propose policies which are important from the labour movement's perspective. The discussions at this conference on technological change indicate to me that a majority actually think that the technology is neutral and are scared to consider fundamental redesign. We have compromised in the face of technological change in the past and we have lost. What does this mean today? It means that we make presentations to the MacDonald Commission that say, "We're not in favour of shorter work time." I'm in favour of shorter work time. The labour movement is in favour of shorter work time. That doesn't mean we can't increase production. What's automation about if it doesn't mean increased production with shorter work time? What we want to talk about is redesigning the work, so instead of producing five million cars that last three years, we produce one million cars that last fifteen years. We're using too much of the world's resources right now. What's wrong with those sorts of ideas? When we sit down with management we never talk about the fundamental things. Every company, including public enterprises set up by social democratic parties, has a five and ten-year plan for development, capital equipment purchase and production totals. How often does the labour movement get access to those sorts of figures? Why isn't labour involved at that stage? Instead of being told that we're going to buy an IBM this or that and asked what colour we want the screen to be, we should talk about what the machine will do and how it is designed. In the face of the reality of the problems, there are really only tiny unions with tiny resources. If you want to sit down with unions and talk seriously about restructuring the workplace, then we have to weight the scale far more heavily on the side of labour.

SCHRECK: You use the shorter work time argument in the context of more voluntary leisure without a cut in real income. Most commonly, shorter work time arguments view work as a scarce commodity. People work less, involuntarily, with a cut in real income to control unemployment. Those are radically different concepts. George Bernard Shaw described socialism as an equal responsibility to work and to receive. As long as there are unmet needs in the world, there is work to be done. While we might cherish an ideal world where we all work only an hour a week, that's not the world we are facing. Right now, we are facing an attempt to impose cuts in real income by making people think that we cannot increase the number of jobs and that therefore jobs have to be rationed. That is the argument we are attacking.

We experimented with Quality of Work Circles in the mid-70s in British Columbia with Resource Boards. We tried a completely decentralized management approach and replaced supervisors with positions that were called team coordinators. In some of those units teams of people worked well together to make the decisions relevant to the functioning of their operation. There was also a real problem. Whenever an individual grievance came up, because all decisions were team decisions, everyone else on the team was opposed to the griever. That put the union in a hell of a position. Team management is like a family or a small town environment: there is tremendous peer pressure to go with the group decision. On the positive side that may mean honouring a consensus in co-operative decision making. On the negative side you really can screw people around a lot. Even under the best of circumstances, when there is no intention to co-opt there are a lot of problems.

NEW VOICE: We conducted a minor experiment in British Columbia with respect to worker directors. We were fortunate in the sense that local people were demanding it from the International Woodworkers of America [IWA] and the government. There was a real response in terms of productivity and ending wildcat strikes, etc. We offered the same opportunity to a so-called more radical union, the Pulp Workers, and they were scared to death of it. I am looking for a more radical restructuring of ownership and control, one that, initially, would look like chaos and anarchy, even to a good many of my friends in the trade union movement. That is a major dilemma for those who want genuine change. I see terribly difficult problems in terms of existing institutional forms and structures within the trade union movement, in terms of responding to major changes in reorganizing our resources industries and regions. Free trade was a good idea, started by the British, which has permeated the educational system down through the decades. We should start to question free trade in terms of the principles we espouse and in terms of the alternative of greater self-sufficiency for all nations of the world.

NEW VOICE: I basically feel that we are fiddling while Rome burns. I also share the basic pessimism. Through a structural quirk, I am associated with the Business Faculty at Simon Fraser University. It is depressing to see the next generation of managers thoroughly inculcated with the belief that management is a profession every bit as hard and tight as medicine or law. To manage you must have at least a Bachelor of Commerce, if not an MBA.

On the other side of the coin, we have inherited a mode of organizing labour that essentially goes back to the 1930s. In the North American context, the *Wagner Act* has absolutely forged our mind set. In 1934, a time of near civil war in a number of American cities, a liberal American senator came up with what is, in effect, the way that 95 percent of us think is the only way that labour can exert its influence. These ideas were codified and transferred into Canadian law.

We are, all of us, victims of our class. Business students think that only people with MBA's can manage. Conversely, on the trade union side, there is a kind of comfort from right, conservative trade unionists who don't want fundamental change and are quite happy to exist within the milieu of collective bargaining as it is specified by the *Wagner Act*. Some on the far left like the fact that it is a straightforward adversarial system. Through all of that, we are optimistically groping for a way in which labour can be a significant fact in management.

NEW VOICE: We should consider a model where the focus is on workers as owners and managers, not in large scale, highly centralized organizations, but in smaller, regional organizations. It is not an attack on unions to take this position. If we are going to maintain the corporate society, there is no question that we have to back the large unions in every way. Unions are the only means by which workers can increase their control. But that doesn't mean that union strength is the only goal. If all socialism amounts to is supporting workers' rights to argue with management, get some input and improve their conditions just a little bit please, it just isn't enough, damn it. We want a heck of a lot more than that. We want the workers in the Kootenays, Smithers, Prince George and Terrace to have control of the operation. I have heard, contrary to a previous opinion, many workers in many places demand a whole lot more. I have heard workers say, "We should take over this show." I heard the Nishga Indians say that they could run the Nass operation. What's missing are the structural conditions that will allow them to do it. There is no question about *what* they could do. We want to reorganize the whole regional operation so that they have the opportunity to do it. If we could get to that point, we would not have large unions, nor would we need large unions. The best way to protect workers' interests is to have the workers controlling the show in the first place. The decentralist argument tries to move toward more genuine democratic control from the bottom.

NEW VOICE: Join the Revolution, Comrades.

NEW VOICE: Unions end up carrying out a defensive manoeuvre. That is fundamentally the nature of the relationship of unions and employers. When we try to formulate the larger programs, such as employment without inflation, we get a negative reaction from many people in unions, and from workers generally, because we do not concentrate on the other side of the equation, on the power of the owners and the managers of the enterprise.

SCHRECK: It is a mistake to link the current inflation problem to either the rate of unemployment or the behaviour of unions. The success of the right wing in doing that has posed many problems for us. Inflation was the result of external shocks which, in any economic model, would have worked their way through to higher prices. OPEC raised oil prices. When the cost of energy goes up, it is not surprising to see the cost of other things go up. The battle to maintain relative shares, on the part of both unions and companies, was a result of adjusting to external shock. If we had simply allowed it to work through instead of destroying programs and creating

massive unemployment by messing around with monetarist
policies, we would have gotten through the shock a lot more
easily. Inflation is a phony issue. We got into an inflationary
cycle as a natural consequence of external shocks to the
economy, not to mention the Vietnam War. Nobody has done
a decent analysis of the effect of the Vietnam War on the
whole inflationary situation: a major war that was financed
without any taxes, by deliberately creating inflation.

We have to consider free trade for two reasons. We have a
responsibility to assume a world view. Are we willing to
improve our living standard by promoting imperialism which
exploits the Third World? Are we willing to rationalize our
exploitation by saying it is not good socialists doing it, it's
those evil multinationals? We have to recognize that, were we
in control, we would still have to deal with the question of
trade with the Third World and the trade off between our
living standard and theirs. More pragmatically, as long as
Canadians export raw materials and have a lot of jobs dependent on them, we can't mess around a whole lot with trading
relationships or we'll be stomped on like a bug, principally by
the U.S. As you may recall, the fiasco we went through as to
whether the U.S. was going to have a tariff on timber exports
quickly pointed out just how vulnerable we are. We have to
accept that as a regrettable but real constraint.

The right wing has been successful in discrediting Keynesianism. It is perhaps dangerous to use that term, but the
fact is that if we want to create more jobs we have to create
the demand for the crap we are going to make, be it services
or products. If we can't sell it, we're not going to employ
people to make it. We have to increase demand and that's all
that Keynesianism is saying. If we accept that we cannot
increase demand and create jobs, we might as well pack it in
and go home. There is no other tool for dealing with the
problem of creating more jobs, which are important for a
variety of reasons not the least of which is that they are the
primary means of income distribution. The ability to do that
depends on the industrial sector you pick. You can pick an
industrial sector where it is guaranteed that you are going to
create more jobs outside your border than within your

border, or you can look for sectors where the opposite is going to be true. Public goods and services are the best areas for expansion in terms of creating the most domestic jobs. There will be political retaliation in the short run through the exchange rate. Undoubtedly part of what happened to Mitterand in France was not the working out of any economic consequences but the fact that opponents of the French government wanted to bring it to its knees and were able to do so by buying and selling francs and driving the exchange rate down. We would undoubtedly come under that same pressure. That has nothing to do with economics. That's international monetary warfare. It is less easy for the States and others to conduct that warfare if the expansion is carried out in such a way that we do not give them more ammunition, i.e., we minimize the leakage so they are not using our own money in retaliation against us, which means choosing sectors, like public education, that leak less as the areas of stimulus.

We have a tendency to dwell on the ownership question to the exclusion of the question "How is our world going to work if we do change ownership?". We will not be prepared to change ownership unless we put into place some of the quality of work ideas that we have discussed. Those ideas are important as a prior condition to a change in ownership. In fact, it is questionable whether changes in ownership are really necessary. Why throw money away repatriating something if we can control it from top to bottom anyway? We have traditionally gotten things very backwards.

It is dead wrong to assume that decentralization will diminish the need for big unions. If we are completely socialized, we will then have groups negotiating with each other. We will still have questions like, "What are the relative wages of woodworkers going to be, relative to the relative wages of brewery workers?". The unions have, and will continue to have, a vital role in negotiating relative wage rates. Part of democratization, decentralization and worker involvement is groups of workers negotiating with each other. That is the role that unions are going to play and big unions are going to have to do that.

PARTICIPANTS' REPORT
The Economy

THE ISSUE
Decentralization

Our society is highly centralized, sexist, racist, hierarchical, and alienating. Our environment is degraded, our resources are wasted. The utility value of work has been entirely subordinated to the exchange value, with the surplus value created by labour being taken by a dominant class and applied to new and increasingly inhumane technologies. Workers take the brunt of capitalist cycles of overproduction and crisis. Metropolitan regions benefit disproportionately as the surplus is directed towards them from hinterland regions.

DISCUSSION

WE SEEK A WAY TO INCREASE the democratic control of the means of production and to avoid capitalist relations of production. We seek a way to increase equality between workers and between men and women. We seek a way to ensure that future technological development is directed by workers toward an organization of work which is humane and creative.

Three alternatives to capitalist assumptions have been advanced by the "traditional" left.

1. State ownership of the means of production;
2. Tripartite negotiations between capital, the state, and organized labour;
3. Worker ownership of the means of production, and organization of political and economic life which includes worker representation in all aspects of industrial enterprises.

The first of these does not necessarily transfer control to workers, and historically has not led to greater democratic control. The state itself becomes the patriarchal authoritarian manager. Tripartite negotiations may involve workers more than at present, but do not transfer control to them and ultimately leave intact both capital and the capitalist state. Worker ownership is a superior objective, but is not without defects. First, workers are also citizens and not all citizens are employed in existing organizations. Women, in particular, are in large part excluded. Secondly, corporate structures remain intact, even if workers ostensibly own them. Thirdly, a change in ownership does not, in itself, solve the problem of in-humane technologies, centralization, predominance of exchange over utility values or regional disparities.

One alternative to the dilemma has more recently been advanced in sufficient detail that we can begin to explore it. This is popularly known as decentralization of the economy and devaluation of the political structure. This refers to smaller *regional* units, with greater *citizen* control of *regional* resources, *social,* in contrast to *state,* ownership; and a technological infrastructure designed to sustain smaller con-centrations of population and to increase their self sufficiency.

Our objective is to discuss the institutional impediments to the transfer of control to the regional level, to make proposals for overcoming these impediments and for implementing a decentralized model, and to state why we view this as the superior direction for the socialist movement.

Corporate Structures and Unions

The present corporate structure places organized labour in large, centralized, hierarchical structures. As these have grown, workers have organized themselves into defensive institutions, large unions. Within the present structures, these unions are the only bulwark against capital, the only institutions capable of representing labour and of protecting labour against increasing subordination and exploitation. Under these circumstances, unions are obliged to prop up and sustain the corporate structure. Union institutional existence is inextricably tied to corporate institutional structure. At best, unions can argue for a decent wage and a reduction in abuses of labour. But built into the system are structural constraints which are antithetical not only to democracy in the workplace but to all fundamental socialist transformations.

Capital-dominated union structures increase wage inequalities and the disparity in both wages and security between unionized employed workers, non-unionized workers and the unemployed. These disparities divide the working class and reduce its collective capacity to alter the system to its collective advantage.

This policy is not directed against trade unions, but rather *toward* the protection of labour. In the short run, unions would lose institutional power, but only insofar as their members, together with unorganized labour, obtain power to control their lives, work, regions, resources and destinies.

The involvement of the trade union movement in the development of the process leading to decentralization and devolution is assumed.

Regional Disparities

Metropolitan regions presently subsist largely on the appropriation of surplus from the resource regions. Consequently, resource regions are chronically and necessarily under-developed. Without control of their wealth, resource regions cannot diversify their economic base. They cannot create and sustain cultural institutions. Communities become transient, company towns destined to become ghost towns when resources are depleted.

Decentralization would stabilize or reduce metropolitan populations. Populations would be dispersed throughout the province, with more towns in the population range of 50,000 to 100,000. Such population dispersion would create demand for diversification of the regional industrial base, which would broaden occupational opportunities. These would lead to greater self-sufficiency and even more regional development. Such towns are large enough to support cultural institutions. The development and implementation of appropriate technologies within these communities would encourage a manufacturing sector.

Gender Inequalities
According to a 1980 ILO report, "women provide two thirds of the world's work hours and produce 44 percent of the world's food supply while receiving only 10 percent of all wages and a mere 1 percent of all property." While the condition of women in the developed countries, and particularly in social democratic jurisdictions, is not reflected in those figures, it is still true that social democratic solutions to the present crisis generally continue to reify such concepts as the economy, production, jobs, work and so forth. The traditional sexual division of labour, which assigns no value to "entropic" work, is not taken into account. Without concerted attack on the division of labour within the family, coupled with strategies such as shorter hours of work, wage solidarity and the rationalization and socialization of household work and child care, the achievement of real sexual equality is impossible.

Decentralization and devolution would require participation and sharing of responsibility by all members of the community, and would introduce a feminist model of collective and consensual decision-making, which is foreign to alienated, hierarchical, centralized institutions.

The Political Context

The achievement of a democratic socialist society requires more than a change of regime. Presently an overadministered, alienated and depoliticized population is viewed by political parties, including social democratic parties, as counters in the game of electoral politics. A new social contract must be founded on the twin concepts of collective participation and collective responsibility.

RECOMMENDATIONS

The Devolutionary Contract

The shift of power to non-metropolitan resource regions of the province should begin through a "devolutionary contract" between the provincial Crown and the regions. The initial contract with all regions would centre on the management of lands within the region, with an emphasis on the public lands. The regions would be responsible for the inventory analysis, planning and management of the land base. Initially there would be some appointees from the province to the regional management structure, and an "extension service" available to the region, but in short order a full electoral process would be established to replace appointed personnel.

The devolutionary contract would require the recognition of the priorities of labour over capital, and emphasize environmental protection, enhancement and renewal.

A second level of devolutionary contract would apply to those more marginal regions that tend to be of limited interest to the corporate power structure. This higher level of devolution would involve the actual transfer of title to the public land base from the province to the new region. This contract also would initially involve an appointive and elective process in the region, and a subsequent electoral process.

This contract would require democratic management of the resources of the region in a manner that was not hierarchical or patriarchal and would be written in the spirit of the Canadian Bishops' "Ethical Reflections" of 1983. The contract would also require that the economic rent of resources and urban land be collected by the region. Initially, this process would require some monitoring by the province. A portion of these rents would have to be returned to the province, and a portion, under the contract, would have to be used to establish new enterprises in the regions, again in the spirit of the Bishops' statement, in a manner that is labour intensive, not capital intensive, energy saving and non-violent.

In "marginal regions" where greater devolution would take place, the province could still be the trustee of lands which have province-wide significance, such as ecological reserves, parks and wilderness areas. Joint provincial/regional management of sensitive trusts could be considered.

Economic Decentralization:
Production and Decision-Making
The most profound economic decentralization would result from a significant redistribution of income. Economic power is, of course, a function of wealth and income assets and this holds true equally for regional decentralization as for decentralization among groups of individuals.

Quantum leaps in communication technology have obviated the need for economic decision-making to be made in a few metropolitan centres. We no longer all need to be in the same place, at the same time, to make significant decisions. We have access to significant information and we can distribute the information with appropriate use of existing technology.

In the public sector, initial moves toward economic decentralization can be achieved through the geographical reassessment of selected government and Crown corporation functions. This phase would be followed by the devolution of certain central government functions to regional and municipal governments. In pursuing a policy of decentralization it will be necessary for central governments to transfer revenue to lower levels of government. The DREE [federal Department of Regional Economic Expansion] experience clearly demonstrates that central bureaucrats are not competent to make development plans for local communities.

Government should also fund local manufacturing endeavours with seed capital. Private sector decentralization should be encouraged through economic arguments and non-coercive moral suasion. Any tax incentives should be negotiated on an enterprise basis. Government negotiators should be contracted from the private sector and paid on a performance basis. Government should encourage private entrepreneurs to follow market incentives rather than tax incentives.

1. Manufacturing
In many industries, optimal utilization of economies of scale can be achieved at production levels lower than those calculated by industry. Secondary processing of primary resources can be located close to the resource sites. High value-added should be a principal objective in the development of processing industries.

2. Ownership and Control
Community participation and industrial democracy should be incorporated in the establishment of local industries. It may be possible to establish co-operatively owned industrial enterprises, particularly in high value-added enterprises. The implementation of an economic decentralization policy demands the exercise of imagination. For instance, forestry workers rendered redundant by technological change may be retrained as skilled fabricators of high quality wood products.

3. Cultural Life
Culture enhances community life. Artistic endeavours are labour intensive, require relatively low initial capitalization and therefore should be encouraged.

Appropriate Technology
The larger socialist strategy of decentralization, urged upon us for political, economic, psychological and ethical reasons, requires the democratic left to take seriously the potential of a technology that would be more accessible and appropriate to self-reliant communities. This is not a simple goal. Improved technology, until very recently, has largely meant changes in scale: megaprojects were the logical outcome. In that sense,

technology is the antithesis of local autonomy and community control.

To reverse this entrenched trend, on even a modest scale, will require, in the words of George McRobie, a "well-organized, systematic and sustained effort." First, the political will to act must be present. Second, the opposition of the beneficiaries of the present system must be anticipated. Third, a serious investment into new kinds of small-scale technologies must be undertaken in some kind of co-operative venture between the provincial government and local communities. Here is an opportunity to exploit recent technological innovation for the benefit of the commonweal. The microchip, the supreme technological achievement in our generation of monopoly capitalism, might ironically be the key tool with which decentralizing socialism can realistically fight back.

In a real sense, after all, the quality of human life is substantially a function of the nature of technology. The work we do, which rightly or wrongly is for most of us the key determinant of our sense of self-worth, is an obvious example.

Gender Relations

A decentralized model which puts utility value and community goals in the foreground, as opposed to exchange value and corporate profit, would foster a value system based on nurturing and co-operation. Such traits have been devalued and marginalized by the institutionalization of traditionally "masculine" values like aggressiveness, competitiveness, individualism. Such a model demands real accountability with respect to production and would recognize the genuine "goods" of a normative, humanistic value system. Within the corporate configuration, services such as child care, health, housing and so forth would be accounted as wealth. Environmental pollution, resource depletion and social inequity would be accounted in the balance sheet as real costs. A social contract which revalues "feminine" qualities, which assumes co-operation, nurturing, egalitarian and democratic norms, would be a first step in the process of breaking down deeply embedded sexist attitudes.

Resource Nurturance and Environmental Concerns

Wherever a small population has subsisted on a limited resource base, it has nurtured and respected the resource and has survived in harmony with its physical environment over many generations. The native people of British Columbia preserved the fishery, the streams and the forests for many centuries. The commercialization of resources and the imposition of mass production technologies increased the demand on resources beyond their replenishment capabilities. As well, industrial waste and low utilization standards are structural components of massive scale production and consumption. Complete utilization and selective resource use is "more expensive" and thus not undertaken.

These are precisely the problems to be overcome through decentralization and appropriate technology. Where a local population controls its own resource base, it has the incentive to preserve it for long-term survival. Such strategies would also increase occupational diversity through greater manufacturing of end use and specialized products. Thus, a policy of economic decentralization leads to greater concern for the environment, greater utilization of resources and greater awareness of human dependence on nature.

Towards Creation of Political Policy

Decentralization has to be a gradual, incremental policy. Regions which are marginal and which can most benefit from change may then become models for the process. But first, politically affiliated social democrats must be persuaded that this policy is the correct one. What is being proposed is a *radical* redirection of the economy and society. The proposal is as much a departure from traditional socialist policies as from capitalist practice. There will inevitably be entrenched opposition from capital and from labour, who have been persuaded by capital to believe that only the present structures can promote well-being and employment. It is vital that a propaganda campaign be developed, first *within* socialist parties, then in the various regions, and ultimately, with gathering momentum, for the entire population.

We advocate therefore, the establishment of:

1. a working group to develop this outline and publish a "working paper";
2. a constitutional law committee to draft a constitution appropriate to the devolutionary society;
3. an educational committee to plan a campaign of information in the workplace;
4. a convention to be undertaken within a year to work out the full ramifications and strategies of this policy.

Decentralization policy should be implemented on a gradual and incremental basis until sufficient popular support exists for its full-scale implementation. This would include:

1. provincial government moves to decentralize some of its own functions to regional boards/towns and give preferential treatment to medium-sized towns;
2. initial attention to marginal areas;
3. extensive public education campaigns on the vital distinction between social or public ownership and state ownership;
4. state expropriation of existing corporations, their properties being turned over to regional populations, as necessary for regional growth.

Nationalizing large industries simply for the sake of nationalization is not the objective. Rather, the objective is to take over industrial and corporate structures which are *necessary* for specific regions.

A Social Contract
The social contract is essentially an economic plan which would project overall growth expectations for the economy and set ensuing guidelines for wages, profits, investment, etc. A supply side public investment policy would seek to reduce costs through expanded production in areas where demand pressure is strong.

A program aimed at bringing about equitable income distribution will require the establishment of a progressive tax system, thus ending the current erosion of the tax base. As well, we would establish an income floor through a Guaranteed Annual Income. Policies consistent with employment and investment objectives would be established to control inflation through exchange and interest policies. As well, selective price controls, especially of utilities and highly monopolized sectors, would be implemented.

Industrial Democracy
The overall goal is to shift power from capital to labour through a process which acknowledges human need and enshrines the principles of justice and equality.

The role of unions is central to any democratic industrial strategy. Innovative ways to expand and strengthen the role of unions must be developed, not only in traditional areas, like the shop floor, but also at higher levels of industrial decision-making, within the firm as well as at the national and provincial levels. Labour should have a voice in the articulation of public wage and investment policy and should be prepared at all levels of organization to address issues like production planning, constraints on capital, and environmental policy.

At the level of the firm, industrial democracy implies worker representation on boards of directors and an expanded mandate for collective bargaining. Issues involving human rights, work-site child care facilities, affirmative action policies in hiring, investment and ownership questions – all should fall within the legitimate scope of union participation. The emphasis on the shop floor should shift to democratization of the work process. The nature and structure of both work and management techniques should be included in the union mandate. Industrial democracy is a creative process whereby workers' experience, skill and knowledge are utilized to determine the nature and structure of jobs.

Although unionized labour will invariably dominate efforts to achieve the goals of industrial democracy, unorganized labour must not be left out. A democratic industrial policy must lobby for legislative initiatives to improve the rights and conditions of unorganized workers and to bring them within the union fold.

Forms of Ownership

There are a number of clear advantages to employee ownership. It encourages decentralization, is more responsive to workers' needs, helps workers understand their relationship to other workers, may improve productivity through reduced alienation, and can provide the opportunity for democratic control in the workplace.

The disadvantages include the risk of inequalities emerging among enterprises and of closure of weaker plants in the face of market or technological change. Two questions need to be resolved: What degree of ownership diversification is possible and practical? What are the implications for industrial relations and the role of unions?

In resource-based industries, governments must oversee an equitable distribution of economic rents, taxes and royalties. Centralized economic planning, presumably carried out by elected councils of workers in similar enterprises, would be necessary for integrated operations. Democratic worker participation in integrated branch plants of multinational companies is not an alternative at this time.

The ownership structure of Crown corporations has many advantages. It provides for public control of natural monopolies and public management of natural resources for public benefit. Industrial democracy strategies to change hierarchical management structures can be implemented in Crown corporations more easily than in privately owned firms.

Worker education in management skills and an exhaustive re-evaluation of the role of unions are prerequisites to achieving enterprises which are owned or controlled or both by unions. The education and evaluation processes would necessarily include determining sources of capital which could be used by employees in acquiring firms. Union pension funds, as well a public and private venture capital, could be used for investment purposes in employee-owned enterprises.

III
THE GOVERNMENT

THE STATE OF THE UNION*

John Fryer
National President
National Union of Provincial Government Employees
Canada

> *A part of the bourgeoisie wants to remedy
> social grievances in order to ensure the stabil-
> ity of bourgeois society. . . They want to have
> the existing society, but without the revolu-
> tionary transferring elements.*
> –Karl Marx, *The Communist Manifesto*

DISCLAIMER: I do not speak for my union or the
trade union movement generally because they have
not yet adopted the progressive policies that I will
outline.

Intense public dislike
Declining membership
Lack of direction
Reduced bargaining rights
Negative collective bargaining

---

* Mr. Fryer's paper "The State of the Union" was presented to a discussion
group which focused on The Government. It is printed here with some
minor revisions.

These are the realities that trade unions face. The trade union movement is on the defensive. During the recent economic recession union membership has stagnated or declined. The International Steel Workers Union lost 750,000 members between 1981 and 1983. Of the 102 unions affiliated with the AFL-CIO, 98 are in decline, four are stable or growing. Many workers laid off in "smokestack" industries are not going to be called back to work.

In fact, the business community has used the recession to automate production work. Technological changes are not designed to recreate former employment levels. A major reason for the decline of membership in many unions is the shift away from employment in the traditionally highly unionized smokestack industries and the growth of employment in high tech and expanding service industries.

While the trade union movement was extremely successful in organizing the Alcans, the Stelcos and the General Motors, we have been notoriously unsuccessful at reaching people who spend their days "interfacing" with video display terminals. Trade unions do influence wages. Bob Kuttner's article "The Declining Middle," published in *The Atlantic Monthly*, notes:

> There is nothing intrinsic in assembling cars, mining coal, or pouring molten steel that requres high wages. These jobs. . . pay well. . . because of the efforts of strong unions.

The corollary is also true. the new service and high tech jobs–fast-food workers, data entry operators, computer assemblers–are non-union and poorly paid.

The unemployment problem is exacerbated by significant demographic shifts in Canadian society. The average age of the population is increasing, while at the other end there is a better educated, younger, more mobile work force, increasingly frustrated because they can't find work. The unions are losing membership, are unable to organize new sectors and have leaders who have little experience with endemic high unemployment. Double-digit unemployment is a given in the forecasts of the Economic Council of Canada and the federal Department of Labour. The end result is that our economy is going to be left with massive, structural, labour force problems for the rest of this decade and, indeed, throughout the rest of this century.

If the labour movement is not in an actual crisis, then it is certainly at a crucial crossroads and we cannot blame all of our ills on external forces. We tend to believe our own bullshit. Once we come up with policies, we don't re-examine them. We have preached a version of Keynesian economics and a full employment policy as the salvation of society. We have to re-examine that policy. An increasing number of voters no longer believes it. We need to go beyond our usual negative knee-jerk responses and talk about reducing working lifetimes, job sharing and part time work. There are worthwhile social and economic goals to be pursued in addition to the goal of full-time full employment. Union leaders may be opposed to part-time work, but there is a growing force of workers who like it. Part-time work and job sharing is coherent with emerging changes in family structure.

Wassily Leontief, Nobel Laureate in economics, proposes that governments supplement the pay of workers who voluntarily cut back to a three-day work week at age 60. Not only would this open up thousands of new jobs for our young people, but those who choose to work fewer hours would suffer no loss of purchasing power. Now, Leontief acknowledges what you are all thinking–this system would be expensive in tax dollars over the short run. but, he argues, as unemployment drops, this mechanism would also generate economic growth and, hence, more revenue.

One thing that still works for unions in Canada, when governments give them a chance, is collective bargaining. Collective bargaining has worked in the past and it can continue to improve the lot of working people, many of whom are not directly affected by the collective agreement. Business, government and labour have key roles to play in this country. One of the roles of government is the establishment of minimum standards for things like health and safety, wages and working conditions. One role for unions is to bargain, cajole and persuade legislators to improve those standards.

In this era of streamlining and downsizing, the trade union movement must make major breakthoughs in non-monetary areas. Issues like health and safety and the establishment of child care centres at the workplace are just two examples. The trade union movement has not adapted to the rapid social changes of recent years. Women, who have been entering the work force at a record rate, do not see themselves proportionally represented on the executive councils of the Canadian labour movement. That may explain why we have not yet won the fight for equal pay and equal opportunity. We have not taken a forefront position in the women's movement. In many respects we have been a hindrance. A growing number of astute, politically conscious women perceive a credibility gap within the union movement.

There was a time when the trade union movement was in the vanguard of the Canadian peace movement. Of the 500 people who attended Operation Dismantle's annual dinner there were two social democratic politicians and three trade unionists. There were a great many young people, especially young women.

Unions and Political Parties

Because the trade union movement is intensely disliked and distrusted thanks in part to media coverage, many social democrats see it as a political Achilles heel. Many union officials think life would be easier if they were free to use the power of members' electoral support when lobbying Brian Mulroney.

This is a very sensitive area. Social democrats and trade unionisits are supposed to have a great deal in common. Social democratic governments are more likely to provide social programs than are right wing governments. There ought to be a natural affinity. Why is it that social democratic parties, when they do win power, frequently manage to annoy public employees? Why do public sector unions succeed in sabotaging social democratic governments?

Over the past fifteen years, social democratic governments in Manitoba, Saskatchewan and British Columbia all started out in office on excellent terms with their public employees. Unfortunately, this initial advantage was not always maintained. Saskatchewan serves as a graphic illustration. the breakdown in communication between 1971 and 1982 was politically disastrous. During the 1971 election, the Canadian Union of Public Employees took a high-profile approach as they battled for a wage catch-up for public employees, especially hospital workers. The campaign was successful and the government began to make good on their promise of a New Deal for People. Wages and working conditions for public employees were dramatically improved. In March, 1982, the Blakeney government moves to renew its mandate. One niggling legislative detail requires attention before the assembly can be dissolved. CUPE hospital workers are on strike. The government brings in legislation on Friday ordering striking employees back to work and announces an election on Saturday.

How utterly ironic that Premier Blakeney, whose government had genuinely done so much for hospital workers, should spend the first week of the campaign facing CUPE demonstrators when entering a public hall. How ignominious that he should find himself embroiled in heated debates with hospital workers who, a decade earlier, thought he walked on water.

What went wrong? I don't know all the answers, but certainly some of them are found in the fact that the new government, having thrown a lot of money at the economic problems of hospital workers, promptly ignored that sector and moved on to nationalize the potash industry, to devise a fairer tax system and to tackle a broad range of pressing social problems. I am not trying to suggest that the Blakeney government deliberately forgot hospital workers, nor that what happened can be blamed on just one side. But by 1982, the upshot was that some advisors to the striking hospital workers were more interested in embarrassing the government than in reaching a negotiated settlement.

Consider the matter of extending French-language services in Manitoba. To its everlasting credit, the Pawley government tried to move this country forward by making

French-language services available in another Canadian province. While the Manitoba government undoubtedly expected resistance from rednecks, I am sure they did not anticipate the storm of criticism that the legislation has engendered. One of the groups to criticize the legislation was the Manitoba Government Employees' Association [MGEA].

The MGEA is not a redneck organization. They have endorsed the notion of practical bilingualism and they support the entrenchment of French-language rights in the Constitution. The MGEA was assured that the legislation in Manitoba was not similar to the open-ended federal system but rather would provide bilingual service to those Manitoba communities where numbers warranted it. Imagine the surprise and chagrin of the MGEA when their lawyers scrutinized the legislation and advised them that the courts would have no alternative but to interpret the legislation as open-ended bilingualism. A failure to communicate, and perhaps more, is involved in both examples of government-employee conflict.

Communication is a two-way street. I don't want to leave the impression that it is always up to a government to take the first step. Public employees, through their unions, should be talking regularly with cabinet ministers and senior government officials about mutual problems and concerns. The exchange of views and ideas between public sector unions and government is always important, but it is critical when the government is a social democratic government. We lack the mechanisms and sometimes the will to ensure good working relations, partially because social democratic parties neglect to establish the ground rules when they are in opposition.

Toward an Income Policy
Social democrats and trade unionists have much in common. Both groups want to create a more equitable tax system. We favour an excess profits tax on major corporations that reap unconscionable profits. We want a surcharge placed on those who receive outrageous and unjustifiable salaries. We want minimum hourly wage rates approved. Social democrats and

trade unionists favour quality government programs and services to the public. We want to see medicare extended, not eroded.

However, there is one policy matter which neither group has adopted and which deserves the closest scrutiny: the development of a plan for the appropriate distribution of income shares among the various groups in society. In short, an Incomes Policy. How you can have a social democratic society without an Incomes Policy is beyond me. However, we are so nervous about the issue that we can't even discuss it on the floor of trade union and party conventions.

Too often Incomes Policy is equated with wage controls, but it is, in fact, far broader. Incomes Policy must take into account prices, profits, salaries, wages, deferred benefits, taxes, tax write-offs and deferred taxes. It means that some sectors of society will have to give something up. Other sectors are going to get something. Those who have, will have to give. Those who do not, will be the recipients. Why that should be so hard for socialists to come to grips with is beyond my comprehension. It is indefensible that Incomes Policy cannot be formally discussed within the institutional structures of social democratic parties and trade union movements. The orthodox conservative wisdom says the issue should not be discussed until electoral success is achieved. The reality is that an Incomes Policy is a prerequisite to electoral success.

An Incomes Policy requires both patience and understanding. It means that all sectors of society have to give up certain things. Trade unions must recognize that, in accepting an Incomes Policy, they will need to readjust to certain realities. Government initiatives which dramatically improve the wages of one beleaguered group in society cannot be taken as a signal for all other groups to use that as a yardstick and leapfrog ahead themselves. Suppose for example, that a social democratic government recognizes that the salaries of nurses have fallen drastically behind other health care workers and decides on an increase of 45 percent over two years. Other groups in the medical field should surely not demand similar percentage increases for themselves. The government was eliminating an anomaly in the system, it wasn't announcing that the Brinks truck was parked at the front steps of the Legislature and that everyone could help themselves to a wheelbarrow full.

What does a trade union receive in return for agreeing to an Incomes Policy? It should be guaranteed that government economic policy does not increase unemployment or interest rates to control inflation. In short, no more monetarism. Workers are entitled to greater involvement in decision-making processes. This implies workers on boards of directors. However, I do not support that concept unless implemented by a social democratic government.

What is an appropriate income share? The extremes of wealth and poverty in our society are literally obscene. Radical solutions are called for. I don't have the magic numbers, but I think the proposal made by Governor General Edward Schreyer, when he was the Premier of Manitoba, has merit. He suggested that the highest paid person in a society should not earn more than three times as much as the lowest paid person.

Incomes Policy is an important national policy which would distinguish us from the old-line parties. Many of us blame our current predicaments on the swing to the right. We forget that Bob Hawke won the Australian election because the electorate was convinced that he could iron out labour-management difficulties and begin national economic reconstruction. At an economic summit following the election, Mr. Hawke was further able to convince labour and business in Australia to agree to an equitable Incomes Policy. Dave Barrett was on the right track in the British Columbia election of 1983 when he proposed the creation of an economic council composed of different groups in society to advise the government on economic policy. Even after such a full discussion I frankly do not know whether the Canadian labour movement would agree to an Incomes Policy but I have a hunch that it would be even harder for a government to convince big business to curb their appetite for huge profits than it would be to convince labour to accept a rational plan for income redistribution.

If the political scales are to be tipped toward social democracy and away from the right, we must face some hard policy issues and must develop straightforwrd, simple, not simplistic, understandable policies.

DISCUSSION

NEW VOICE: I congratulate you on what you are saying with respect to an Incomes Policy. During a recession, unfair income distribution is made even worse. In Manitoba, the government informed public sector unions that there was no more than $50 million available for wage increases in the 1983-84 fiscal year. Our policy is that the lowest income levels should get the majority of the money. A group of university professors settled a two-year contract at rates that will give then $2,500 in the first year and $2,000 in the second, on an average annual salary of $42,000. We have 81,000 public servants. If everyone received similar increases, we would have spent three times what we have in our pot. Those who have, are not prepared to make concessions on the basis that in times of recession, when the total production of goods and services declines, there will be relatively less purchasing power for lower income people.

NEW VOICE: The issue of Incomes Policy is complicated because we have split jurisdictions in Canada. Most labour relations are under provincial jurisdictions. Taxes, interest rates, price policies in the energy field and most things that influence unemployment and compel people to have more real income are controlled by Ottawa. How do we deal with that and still make sense of an Incomes Policy? I can see Ottawa screwing every provincial social democratic government that attempts to develop an Incomes Policy or social contract, either deliberately or by pursuing poor economic policy in areas like energy and interest rates.

FRYER: Until trade unions and social democratic parties are prepared to develop a policy, that question is premature.

There are politically expedient responses to that problem. Provincial jurisdictions can influence interest rates through mortgage rebates and subsidies on gasoline. Right wing parties come up with these programs and buy themselves elections. We don't. We must develop the policies first. Just having the debate would be tremendously valuable. There are no easy solutions but we must be seen to be coming to grips with some of these tough questions even if we can't reach instant agreement.

I talk to guys in pubs who ask why we have to pay the world price for oil if we've got so much of the stuff under the ground. That's a hard debate to get into. International vulnerability is real and complex as are the jurisdictional problems, but there are also certain fundamental principles. Canadians can be convinced that we shouldn't be paying the same price for oil as countries that don't have the resource. Why should we pay the same money for energy as the Japanese when that price structure gives them a competitive advantage which takes away Canadian jobs.

NEW VOICE: The CLC has begun to back away from the traditional idea that full employment means 1,900 hours of work per year per worker, but that has taken a long time. However, in the near future governments may not have the resources to solve the problem of redistribution of income. Looking for means to redistribute income other than through government involvement reveals another sacred cow. Thirty hours work for 40 hours pay is a great slogan. However, a reduction in work hours is probably going to mean a reduction in real wages. The choice is whether we take from people who have, in terms of real wages, in order to give work to people who are currently unemployed, or whether we try to create new full employment. That is one of the dilemmas that should be addressed here.

FRYER: The resources are limited and the trade offs are real. Universality of social programs is another sacred cow that is exposed when we confront the fact that limited resources may prevent governments from addressing redistribution problems. Universality made sense in the post-Depression era. Perhaps it doesn't make sense today. Perhaps Canadians wouldn't go crazy if readjustments were made to the family allowance system. The resources have to come from somewhere. The problem of income redistribution will not be solved through transfer payments. The issues are deep-seated. They have been with social democratic parties and the trade union movement since the Depression and they are not going to move or bend or be revised easily. I am making a plea for serious dialogue to begin. It took two years to get the CLC to hold a conference on technology. People wanted to pretend that the new technology was going to go away. It's here and it's not going away. But you have to start to talk before you start to find solutions.

The role and size of government are two more sacred socialist cows from which we retreat while the right advances and takes the whole ground. Government liquor stores are an antiquated, bizarre and socially unacceptable way of distributing liquor. There are services that do not need to be under direct provincial government control. We can change the role of government without putting people out of work. Vancouver Resource Boards are a classic example of social democratic decentralization which was well received by the recipients of social services. We get trapped by our own rhetoric. I predict that a Conservative government in Ontario will adopt decentralized delivery of welfare services.

NEW VOICE: In that instance our rhetoric may not be a trap. The right is still debating the merits of decentralizing welfare services. The Fraser Institute did a study for Sterling Lyon and even they said it was a dumb idea.

NEW VOICE: The neo-conservatives argue that high government deficits preclude social program spending. The idea that governments cannot afford social programs because we are living beyond our means is an absolute myth. It ignores the fact that present Canadian industrial capacity is grossly under-utilized. The potential productive economy could generate 20 percent more than what it is currently producing.

For 1982 and 83 that meant foregone revenues of about $40 billion. The notion that full employment may no longer be a desirable goal is troublesome. The Economic Council of Canada, among other groups, has redefined full employment from 3 percent to 6 percent to 12 percent. But we can have full employment without number-juggling. It is a question of how to achieve it. Possibly reducing the work week and work sharing schemes are good ways of doing it. There is no reason, with the right mix of fiscal and monetary policy combined with some structural policies, that we cannot have full employment.

Unions are not in the vanguard of important social issues because they are just another interest group. Their primary function is to maximize wages. That is why there is a conflict between social democratic governments and unions. The social democratic government's agenda is obviously very different. Is it, therefore, right to pose the dilemma of government in terms of conflict with unions and the public sector? However, that is not a high priority question. The high priority question is the role of government. These issues have been raised by the new conservatives. Some of the arguments that the damn Fraser Institute makes have validity. Bureaucrats do maximize their power and the size of government by instituting social programs which do not redistribute income but which create high paying jobs for social workers. Politicians tend to respond to narrow interest groups. To some extent the very nature of electoral politics makes it impossible for governments to operate in the public interest and certainly in a social democratic interest. Social democratic governments should dramatically reduce the role of government, not in the way the neo-conservatives suggest, but by removing programs and subsidies which benefit very powerful corporations and other powerful interest groups in our society. We should take the neo-conservative agenda and use it to our advantage. We may end up with a lot more successful society.

NEW VOICE: The size of government does need to be curtailed. The neo-conservative strategy is blatantly anti-union. "Downsizing" by a government like the Social Credit in British Columbia can have one of two results. The union will either be weakened to the point that it will be wiped out or it will be strong enough to stand up and fight. There is no middle ground. Those are the alternatives: a donneybrook or surrender. Social democratic parties should be very concerned with building a good working relationship with public sector unions because the chances of an intelligent and rational discussion and electoral success would be immeasurably better as a result of such a relationship.

THE GOVERNMENT AND THE WELFARE STATE*

DISCUSSION

PLOTKE: Increasingly, the welfare state is seen, not as a solution to, but as the source of, economic, social and political problems. Similar arguments against the welfare state, can be heard in the U.S., Britain and, to a lesser extent, Canada. In the United States, conservative criticism developed from a relatively narrow political spectrum. The narrow, hard right which is opposed to any form of welfare statism has widened and softened to speak as the new common sense. It is politically acceptable to view the social programs of the 60s and 70s as undesirable. It is less acceptable to attack the programs of the 1930s–social security and unemployment insurance. The left, in responding to Reagan, has not been very sensitive to this distinction.

The conservative critique is a coherent attack which has gained substantial popular support because it is not completely wrong. The view of the state as bureaucratic and inefficient is consonant with people's experiences. The left has not engaged in analysis which challenges ideology and therefore must often defend programs primarily because the right has taken the initiative. The conservative critique is

* Prof. David Plotke chaired a discussion group which focused on The Government and the Welfare State. A summary of Prof. Plotke's views can be found in Part II, "Recasting Economic and Social Policies."

populist not elitist. It does not speak as an explicit desire to transfer resources to the wealthy. To say that conservative policies merely serve the rich is an inadequate political response.

NEW VOICE: I sense some tension between you and Mr. Wachtel's discussion of the international monetary system.* Your paper, "The Future of Social Policy,"† suggests that autonomous national social policies are possible.

What about a profit squeeze created by social policies, especially regarding regulatory measures? The conservative view is not simply wrong: profits did decline in the 1970s, and an increased social wage and regulatory pressures played a role. But the real question is whether or not there exist adequate funds for renewed investment at profitable rates (or if they are not immediately on hand, whether such funds could be made available through means other than cutting the social wage).

The core of a response should be an insistence that a "reasonable" rate of profit is socially determined, and that across nations no automatic relation exists between that rate and the rate of investment. Nor is there a simple relation between state (social) spending and economic growth. Any notion of a zero-sum situation in which reduced profits necessarily reduce investment concedes far too much rationality to the operation of American capitalism. Perhaps a hydraulic relation would exist if the entire economic mechanism were taut, with no wasted resources, under-utilized skills, or ineffective forms of management. This is far from the actual economic situation in the U.S. New

* See Wachtel's presentation in Part IV, The World.

† David Plotke, "The Future of Social Policy: A Response to the Conservative Critique of the Welfare State," paper prepared for the Boag Foundation conference on Challenges to Social Democracy in the Eighties and Beyond.

investment funds are actually and potentially available without slashing federal spending on welfare.

Given the transnational nature of the world economy, how far are you prepared to stick by this point and defend it?

PLOTKE: Control of social policy has not been taken out of the hands of the nation state by the power of the transnational economy. There are severe but not absolute constraints. Research data does not indicate a definite negative correlation between levels of social spending and rates of profit and investment.

NEW VOICE: I agree. We should not be spooked by the magnitude of transnational influences to the point that we feel we have no room to manoeuvre. How do we translate economic arguments for social spending into terms that touch people's values?

PLOTKE: There is always a delicate balance between efficiency and humanity arguments. The left speaks for the humanity arguments. The right makes the efficiency argument and beats the left over the head with it. The left could more effectively connect the two. Unemployment is not only a terrible individual fate, but a terrible waste of national productive resources.

NEW VOICE: In Canada, we have played around with the idea of a guaranteed annual income for a long time. My hunch is that it is no longer on the agenda because nobody believes the resources are available. Is a guaranteed annual income a sensible component of a social policy which addresses the changing relationships between jobs, income and family structure?

PLOTKE: A guaranteed annual income platform would be a good way to lose an election in the U.S. Instead, the appropriate policy instruments will be indirect, revolving around job training and family policy. Implicitly the basis of social policy has been to find ways to support traditional nuclear family units supported by a male wage earner. Unemployment statistics used to be reported as the proportion of married men out of work. The core assumptions have changed. Women now have a claim on jobs. The number of people who consider themselves legitimately entitled to employment has expanded and will continue to expand quite steadily. A more serious, social policy problem results from families headed by female wage earners because single women frequently do not earn enough money from their jobs to provide child care and support their families.

The old family form has broken apart. Policy instruments which respond to the new situation have yet to be developed. They will be of two types. The first will involve job sharing arrangements and different conceptions of who deserves a job and what kind of job. Secondly, social policy must concern itself with child care and family assistance.

NEW VOICE: The morality critique of the conservatives could be emphasized. The argument that welfare creates dependency is not incorrect but the rise of fundamentalism contains a much stronger critique of the welfare state based on morality. The split between the neo-conservatives and the hard right which maintains the ethic of personal salvation splits the old liberal coalition into those who believe in equal opportunities and those who believe in equal results. Would you suggest that social democratic parties should abandon equal results as a platform and develop an electoral coalition around the protection of equal opportunity?

PLOTKE: Equal opportunity does not appear to ground social policy very effectively. However, in order to affect social policy grounded in equal results, the electoral community must have a positive notion of politics and government. The moral argument can be countered only by policies which address the reality of dependency. If you cannot argue that government interference in social welfare does not necessarily create dependency, you are backed up into the problem of opportunity vs. the problem of result.

NEW VOICE: If we accept that the right has taken the initiative and gained the political advantage our view is pretty gloomy. We have restricted our discussion to the U.K., the U.S. and Canada, and yet results in recent elections elsewhere give a little more hope. Progressive parties have taken the initiative in Sweden, Australia, France, Spain, Greece and Portugal.

PLOTKE: I confess that I am caught in the American thing. I live there. I'm not so gloomy about what's possible. I do insist that the American and British experience suggests that social democrats should consider the right's arguments more carefully. The left remains reluctant to really figure out why the right has been able to make these arguments effectively on a mass popular level. If they were just persuading the rich and a handful of the middle class about the truth of the virtues of selfishness they would not have won so many elections.

NEW VOICE: Excuse me. Reagan got 28 percent of the vote in 1980. Carter got 24 percent. The rest stayed home.

PLOTKE: In the U.S. if you were going to move things to the left you would have to mobilize non-voters and persuade them to vote on the left. And it is possible to do so. That is a far cry from saying that the non-voters are a reserve army of leftists sitting at home waiting for a better candidate. Reagan did get only 28 percent of the vote, but working class and poor people did not feel sufficiently compelled to vote against someone who was openly attacking unions and social welfare programs. In Britain, in a genuine three-party race, Thatcher got 42 percent of the vote, which in European politics is very good. Parties who get that percentage normally stay in power for a long time.

NEW VOICE: I must comment on the difference between Canadian and American political discourse, not to convince you that our discourse is better or more advanced but simply to emphasize that there is a difference. Over the years the left in Canada has successfully advanced specific social policies. We have achieved medicare. Canadian discourse with regard to economic policies is quite different. We have nationalized hydro-electric, air line, railroad and broadcasting systems. Clumsily or otherwise, we have managed to include a class element, as well as an economic element, in our discourse. Despite the similarities, with these differences, are our experiences comparable?

PLOTKE: The difference is substantial. Nowhere in the United States do people who are even close to power talk about the kinds of policies that are proposed here. In the U.S. such things are exclusively academic concerns. Left leaning elected officials in the United States do not use the word socialist. They are economic democrats, progressives, or liberals. There are real and complex differences and I hope that the benefits of those differences continue to accrue to the people of Canada. However, to be provocative, Britain, which is more similar to Canada than to the U.S., has a ferociously monetarist and right wing populist government. The differences which exist might mean that Canada's version of right wing government would be particularly vehement. Reagan did not do, nor is he about to do, what the Social Credit government in British Columbia is trying to do. The difference in discourse is acknowledged, but that difference doesn't guarantee immunity from ferocious right wing policies.

NEW VOICE: Provincial and national social democratic parties in Canada have a smug reliance on a bedrock socialist vote that is disintegrating precisely because conservative policies are starting to make sense to the electorate. Polling for the 1984 federal election indicated precisely that in an alarming way.

PARLIAMENTARY DEMOCRACY ON THE ROPES*

Roy Romanow
Former Attorney General
Government of Saskatchewan

Is PARLIAMENTARY DEMOCRACY ON THE ROPES? Is it something that socialists should save from impending death? That is a complex and difficult question. There is much evidence to suggest that parliamentary democracy is imperilled. Certainly its relevance is in question. Political decisions are not being made by Members of Parliaments and Legislative Assemblies. With some notable exceptions, legislative debates are unenlightened and boring. Many people feel that their participation, mainly by voting in infrequent elections, is too indirect and ineffective to grant any legitimacy to parliamentary democracy. The rise and size of Operation Solidarity in British Columbia indicates a felt need for extra-parliamentary action. The attempt to impose restraint legislation is seen as illegitimate

---

* The article "Parliamentary Democracy on the Ropes?" is an edited transcription of Mr. Romanow's presentation to the discussion group which focused on The Government.

because the program was not disclosed or debated prior to implementation.

The electorate's perception of the role of government is problematic for parliamentary democracy. During the current economic recession, it has become evident that the average voter no longer sees government and its instruments as positive forces in society. This marks a change from the Great Depression when the villain was perceived to be the private market system, and programs such as Roosevelt's New Deal were seen as instruments of economic and social salvation. In Canada, the Co-operative Commonwealth Federation came very close to gaining power in Ontario in 1943, and in 1944 they took office in Saskatchewan. Fifty years later, the average person sees government's bloated bureaucracies, staggering deficits, and unimaginative programs as major problems. Governments, and indirectly parliament and parliamentary processes, are rejected and, therefore, are in crisis.

Can we abandon the parliamentary system? What are the alternatives? The American system divides responsibilities between executive, legislative and judicial arms. Following this model, power could be shifted to enable an executive judiciary system of government. The entrenched Charter of Rights may be edging Canada in this direction. Certainly in the United States the courts, through the interpretation of the Bill of Rights, tend to be an alternative or parallel government. Austria provides a corporatist model where government is, by agreement, among associations that represent powerful interest groups. I come down solidly on the side of parliamentary democracy as the best vehicle to provide accountability, responsibility and representation. As socialists we should believe in people using the state to realize our goals. We believe in an active not a passive state. If we want an active state we need a system that assumes accountability to people and government. Despite all its weaknesses, if done well, parliamentary democracy permits more accountability than the U.S. congressional system, an executive judiciary system, or a corporatist consensus-seeking system.

How do we make the parliamentary system run well? An obvious thrust would be to emphasize the relevance of individual legislators. Elected representatives need more freedom, fewer votes where non-confidence applies, and more resources to research their positions. Canada should look to the example of the American Office of Technical Assistance. Political parties have an obligation to reform their administrative and financial structures. Parliament needs to be more reflective of the minority groups in our country and less the old boys' club that it really is.

It is important for socialists in Canada to be conscious of the fact that our parliamentary system must work within a peculiar brand of federalism. Canadian federalism applies to a unique country of only 25 million people, the majority of whom are within a hundred miles of the American economic and cultural giant. We are a very regionalized nation. The first such federation was the United States and perhaps the most left wing of the American revolutionaries was Jefferson. He believed that all people should be able to participate as directly as possible in government and that government should be accountable to the people. Jefferson proposed decentralization of legislative authority to state and local governments and mistrusted the power of the appointed judiciary. Ironically, and despite John A. MacDonald's *British North America Act* [BNA], Canada has come closer to approaching Jefferson's ideal than has the U.S. Unlike the United States, we have strong provincial governments and relatively strong municipal governments that can undertake major projects of reform. Federalism allowed Saskatchewan to institute medicare. The assignment of legislative powers allowed the provincial government to take over the potash industry.

Since confederation, there have been fluctuations in the federal system between centralization and trends to decentralization. Pierre Trudeau's Liberal government's fear of both Quebec separatism and, to a lesser extent, strong western provincial governments resulted in a shift to centralization. The new *Canada Act* may potentially upset the Jeffersonian principles of local control. The popularity of the Charter of Rights reflects public mistrust of parliamentary political process and indicates a willingness to trust the judicial as opposed to the political process. The Cruise Missile and the Borowski abortion cases are evidence of this trend. I am very surprised by the number of socialists who are willing to allow the courts to establish policy. The inherent philosophical contradictions should become clear if you consider arguments surrounding the entrenchment of property rights. Few socialists are willing to allow the courts to interpret property rights. Why then should we trust the courts to interpret all sorts of other fundamental issues? In my judgment, the same contradictions exist with respect to federalism. Does a socialist choose to support the *Canada Health Act* because it defends medicare against trends such as those in evidence in Alberta? We cannot have it both ways. We like our loose federalism when it spawns medicare in Saskatchewan but we don't like it when it spawns a Lougheed in Alberta with extra-billing.

As democratic socialists, we must support and enhance the principle of parliamentary democracy because it provides accountability and the easiest route to effective action. The parliamentary system and federalism are flawed and under pressure. Socialists would do well to resuscitate those institutions through a recommitment to the concepts and notions of federalism in accordance with the underlying theme of decentralization and devolution.

PERVASIVE PRACTICAL PROBLEMS*

Evan Simpson
Department of Philosophy
McMaster University
Hamilton, Ontario

THE COMMON THEME, VARIOUSLY EXPRESSED as diffusion of control, decentralization, devolution of power, consultative processes, concerns about the size of government, and the power of individual MPs and MLAs as opposed to cabinets has important implications. It suggests a shift away from the Canadian left's strong support of central government and our flirtation with some version of state socialism. What we are saying is much more strongly pluralistic. This opens up the heart of politics because it applies politics directly to the people's values. We are moving away from fancy abstractions toward a position which emphasizes listening to what people have to say.

* The article "Pervasive Practical Problems" is an edited transcription of Prof. Simpson's presentation to the discussion group which focused on The Government. His paper "Prospects for a Moral Economy" is available from the Boag Foundation.

Devolution, decentralization and diffusion imply a strong commitment to democracy. These principles express confidence in the ability of people to reach practical conclusions collectively. We express profound commitment to equality because real democratic consultation diminishes the power of special interests. We also begin to state a solution to the pervasive practical problems which we have always faced. The difficulty of arriving at solutions is evident in some of the papers we have heard. Wachtel* tells us how to deal with the current international monetary crisis, but he doesn't tell us what happens after that. Plotke gets a little fuzzy when it comes to the real practical implications of what he has to say. Baum seems to hope for a miraculous transformation of human consciousness. None of these discussions really describes a vision of a transition to socialism. Practical devolution of power and decentralization requires direct mechanisms to build the expectation of consultation into the political fabric of the country. This expectation defines a socialist vision which, once entrenched, can only subject the power of money to popular control. Obviously, I am describing something that could happen only over a long period of development and evolution, but it is the kind of development we can understand and promote, expressed in terms which describe long-term interests in a way that is intelligible to the public.

The necessity of the consultative process in a socialist vision provides a clear answer to the recurrent question. Do we favour Incomes Policy? An Incomes Policy requires precisely the kind of consultation we are discussing. Such a policy could work only if everybody, including the unorganized, unions, business and women, is involved in the discussion. The implication of such a policy is a vast opening up of political process. It means a massive diffusion of government. It means, if we look at it seriously, a revised conception of parliamentary socialism. Such a policy tends to undermine the special privileges that business interests have by affirming

* See Prof. Wachtel's "Transnational Economy and Social Democracy" in Part IV.

that the division of individual income and profits is a matter of social decision. It encourages stability and corresponds to some of the deepest human values. For this reason particularly, it is eminently politically salable. It represents the highroad of non-confrontation and, at least outside British Columbia, we know the Canadian attitude to confrontation. It robs the right of the rhetoric of restraint and blunts the big labour argument. It enables social democratic parties to persuasively broaden their representative base. Obviously there are enormous complications in working out the details of an Incomes Policy in particular and the modes of diffusion and decentralization more generally. If we focus on decentralization and diffusion, we have a good handle on the strategies that we are responsible for developing.

DISCUSSION

NEW VOICE: What would prevent the well organized, the wealthy and the powerful from monopolizing the consultative process at the expense of the unorganized, the poor, the powerless?

SIMPSON: We must find ways to give genuine capacity to all relevant groups to make their case. This problem was well demonstrated at the Carter Commission where business interests were so fantastically overrepresented that the excellent submissions by the labour movement were overwhelmed. Appropriate mechanisms to create equity in discussion would probably have to include financial support.

NEW VOICE: Are you suggesting that an Incomes Policy would lead to the diffusion of power? Austria's Incomes Policy is the oldest and most highly developed model and it suggests that the process of refereeing an Incomes Policy results in a centralization of power.

SIMPSON: An Incomes Policy implies a diffusion of power in the sense that the decisions of government no longer represent the edicts of a party alone, rather they necessarily express all the points of view that have been fed into the whole process. In one respect that is an extension of the way in which the country is governed. I recognize that it could be described in an opposite way. In bringing it together into a network of discussion, we are disestablishing part of the apparatus of collective bargaining that is located in local unions, but that is better described in terms of making the process coherent.

NEW VOICE: Ever since the publication of *Social Planning for Canada*, the left has relied on central government and the parliamentary system to reform our society. The increasing recognition of the real limits of the government to deliver and inform society and the increasing awareness that the conservative critique of large government has a lot of validity is encouraging. All social democrats should read Milton Friedman's *Capitalism and Freedom* and think seriously about his arguments. We have been defending big government and social programs that we did not really create. We should be taking the offensive by developing specific policies for decentralization of power, worker democracies, cooperatives, and innovative institutions and social programs.

I am theoretically optimistic, but I am also very pessimistic because I have virtually no concrete examples of elected social democratic governments in Canada actually doing any of this. They haven't wanted to give up centralized power. In Saskatchewan there was little effort to get workers involved in running the Potash Corporation. There is a tendency once elected to maintain centralized power. How can we ensure that once elected we will begin implementing some of these ideas?

NEW VOICE: The neo-conservative dominance of information technology as applied to polling techniques may defuse social democratic policy initiatives on decentralization and consultation. They use polling to create an illusion of consultation. Within the constraints of its very simple nature, two-way electronic polling does give people opportunities to have input. However, the technology as applied does not deal with the whole social context or involve opportunities for growth in a collective way which reflects the fact that we live in communities and not separate wired boxes.

ROMANOW: I sympathize with the underlying assumption of fear which motivates your comment. There is an appeal to facile consultative democracy which amounts to little more than electronic inquiries regarding political and consumer preferences and perspectives. All political parties will have to resort to this tactic to some extent. In Saskatchewan we were incredibly naive not to attempt to assess public impressions and involve ourselves with public consultation. In practical political terms the negative impact was evident in the last election. I am a committed political party person. I conceive of consultation through a social democratic party comprised of men and women who hold certain economic and social objectives. The party must embrace the poor, the unemployed, Indians and women. There are no perfect solutions. We are, after all, only frail human beings. It isn't even a matter of executive dominance. It becomes a matter of administrative and technological dominance. However, we must continue to work toward an open political process, use modern techniques of polling where necessary, and hope that the constituent elements of the political party are strong enough to keep us heading in the left direction.

NEW VOICE: Some of our discussion indicates that we may be unwilling to declare our commitment to parliamentary democracy. There is no overt disagreement, but perhaps we are engaging in self-gratification. It smacks of setting up a straw man so as to knock him down. We are very eager to talk about political power, decentralization, devolution, massive and continuous consultation without declaring the fundamental principles which will give expression to this. This tendency is evident in our ambivalence toward the Charter of Rights. My jury is out on the Charter of Rights as such but a Constitution, which, parenthetically, we have never really had in a Canadian social democratic party, necessarily defines where the locus of sovereignty should lie. If sovereignty rests with parliament, then parliament establishes the consultative rules. If sovereignty lies with people, then parliament is an instrument. Parliamentary sovereignty and popular sovereignty are large generalities, but they state the problem which socialists have to be able to solve, particularly in this country. Some of the ground rules have to be constitutionalized and put out of the reach of legislators because legislators work on the basis of the majority and we have minorities who will never accept that ground rule. If we are really serious about consultation, we are going to have to go beyond merely seeking opinion, or facilitating the expression of opinion, or providing more money, or more research. We are going to have to balance parliamentary sovereignty with popular sovereignty and give the citizenry a chance to vote in as many ways and as often as we can. I don't want to be consulted; I want to vote. As democrats we have to go in that direction. I have heard it said that democratic socialists hold the principle of parliamentary democracy as a fundamental tenet–well I don't. I believe in parliament but I believe the people are supreme. That is where the sovereignty lies.

NEW VOICE: Northrup Frye contends that economics tends to centralize culture. The NDP government in Saskatchewan tried to pursue a cultural policy particularly with regard to cable TV. Can provincial, as opposed to federal, governments determine policy in cultural areas?

ROMANOW: The pressure of technology–the global village –makes it very difficult for provinces to play a large role in constructing cultural policy. We seem to be incapable of circumventing arguments which say central management of technology is necessary and that a national cultural position is the best defence against American cultural imperialism.

NEW VOICE: I am not certain we really believe in devolution through a pluralistic socialism. Our uncertainty is apparent in relation to Incomes Policy. There is a tendency to see Incomes Policy as the panacea of the new economic policy. Incomes Policy does seem to imply centralization. In a sense we have an Incomes Policy in this country which has devolved through local unions and local businesses bargaining with each other. Given the nature of Canadian federalism and the powerful positions of the provinces, I'm not sure that we want to completely abandon that model. The thrust of devolution is correct, but we must match that with more traditional views about central planning and state intervention in the economy. Without that balance, we will have two sets of nice slogans which won't match up and won't do us a hell of a lot of good.

NEW VOICE: We have two sets of principles: central planning at the provincial and federal level and devolution/decentralization of power which is more than superficial consultation. Can someone who has held the reigns of state power give specific examples where that conflict was addressed?

ROMANOW: At the present time the balance of power between federal and provincial jurisdictions is fairly good. We have to maintain the principles of economic union. If we gain office federally, we have to have sufficient economic leverage to do something.

PARTICIPANTS' REPORT
The Government

THE ISSUE
Distribution of Powers

There is an alarming trend towards centralization at every level of government and the economy. In many cases, this trend is undemocratic and anti-human and should be resisted. Alternatives must be proposed to increase the involvement of all segments of the community, the organized as well as the unorganized. It must also be recognized that certain activities are best performed on a more centralized basis.

DISCUSSION

THE ACHIEVEMENT OF POLITICAL RIGHTS has led to some modification, but not to fundamental change, of the way economic power is exercised in our society. The basic rights of employers to hire and fire and to direct the corporation on behalf of the shareholders has remained largely unchallenged despite the increasing impact of these decisions on workers, communities, the environment and consumers.

Technology, neutral in itself, has become a centralizing force in our society. There has been a rapid centralization of government power with many more decisions being made at the cabinet level. Local decision-making powers, for example of school boards and community boards, are being taken away and vested in cabinet.

Centralization of economic power leads to centralized government. At the same time the power to plan and control the economy is being turned over to large corporations in the name of the free market. Other aspects of life are also being centralized. Control of the media and cultural activities is being directed from Ottawa and provincial capitals.

RECOMMENDATIONS

To give workers and communities more opportunities to participate in the management of economic units, social democratic governments must challenge the way economic power is exercised. This could be accomplished through the creation of new publicly owned industries; legislative initiatives which grant selective public control of economic decisions on a regional basis; and government takeovers of ownership. A campaign for economic democracy must be central in the socialist vision. The priorities of human ends and human goals in the management of the economy must be stressed.

Elements in a Program of Economic Democracy

- increased worker influence through reform of labour legislation, including the right to organize;

- regular and comprehensive information for workers about the enterprise or organization where they work;

- a comprehensive process of workplace democracy, to extend to all firms with more than 25 employees;

- implementation of workplace democracy as a condition of tax incentives and government grants and contracts, including the unorganized workplace;

- increased corporate efficiency and responsiveness through more supervisory functions performed by the work force;

- legislative provisions for equality in the workplace;

- substantial worker representation on corporate boards or decision-making bodies at the local (plant), intermediate (firm or subsidiary), and national (parent company) levels;

- representation from the community on boards of directors and decision-making bodies at the local level;

- application of models of economic democracy to government agencies, departments and crown corporations;

- provision of information and training in skills of co-ownership and economic democracy for workers.

- provision of information and research to reinforce the community's claim to power;

- control of pension funds and government investment funds as a tool for worker input and control over corporate decisions;

- provision for elected or appointed community resources to oversee local delivery of provincial/ federal services;

- inclusion of workers and trade union representatives as integral parts of government agencies, boards and commissions;

- development of employee investment funds using excess profits to transfer economic power from shareholders to workers and communities.

THE ISSUE
A Social Contract for Canada

DISCUSSION

Investment, production and income distribution decisions should be the result of *social* decisions, rather than capital or free market decisions. The state or government should not act alone in making these decisions. We reject the state socialism model. Government acts as a guardian of the public interest, as defined through open processes of consultation and negotiation.

Economic Goals
The concept of a "social contract" crystallizes much of the appropriate role of a social democratic government. The "social contract" involves a process of making decisions regarding:

1. economic planning (particularly planning of investment, and the distribution of national income between consumption and investment);
2. distribution of income and wealth between individuals and classes;
3. determination of levels of collective consumption (i.e., share of resources directed to the welfare state).

A social contract also involves the creation of institutions and/or informal mechanisms which emphasize co-operation and compromise between capital, labour and government. Fighting for a social contract will bring the integrative goals of democratic socialism to the forefront, and means must be developed to mobilize and involve the unorganized. The precise content and institutional form of a national or provincial social contract must be negotiated and suited to particular circumstances, and cannot, therefore, be spelled out in great detail. However, the Austrian system is an example which deserves study.

As socialists, we cannot accept the "Incomes Policy" implicit in a capitalist society. We feel that income distribution and levels of income must be determined by bargaining at a more global level than by company or industry.

A social contract can work only if there is open, public access to corporate fiscal and planning records.

The logic of a social contract relationship will lead to increased public support for explicitly socialist goals (e.g., democratic control of the investment process and the workplace, egalitarian distribution of income and the enhancement of social consumption).

Social Goals

In striving for a universally decent society, socialist governments must value the independence of the individual and resist the authoritarian tendencies which seduce big government. A socialist government must care about and have an image of caring about people. We must do this through policy which encourages full opportunity to grow in non-work time. Leisure must be universally accessible, with the eventual goal of eliminating cost barriers to leisure time and activities. Correspondingly, governments must support the wide dissemination of culture. A socialist government must eliminate violence to the environment.

RECOMMENDATIONS

Independent and politically affiliated social democrats, along with the labour movement, must consider and debate the terms of a social contract as a matter of immediate importance.

THE ISSUE
Government Structure

Current government structures have contributed to a low level of public confidence in institutions of government.

DISCUSSION

Parliamentary democracy must remain the basic political structure through which the Canadian social democratic movement must work. Canadian reality demands a tension between centralization (intervention) and decentralization (devolution) of power.

Within existing institutions social democrats should work to enhance a legitimate balance of interests in opposition to executive power. Reforms to the parliamentary and electoral system should establish fewer votes of confidence and increase the power of the individually elected members and parliamentary committees through increased financial and staff support. Social democratic parties should explore a proportional representation system within the context of continued territorial constituencies.

While the Charter of Rights is a method for devolving executive power, parliament, however, must not transfer its sovereignty to the courts. Rather, power must devolve upon the citizens. Regarding an amending formula, although the Charter of Rights and the Constitution have found acceptance among most governments, greater political legitimacy will be realized only by the expressed consent of the people of Canada. The Charter of Rights is neither a panacea for socialists nor a substitute for democratic processes.

RECOMMENDATIONS

Crown Corporations
Crown corporations provide a method of devolving power and a method for experimenting with economic democracy. They must have genuine autonomy, with the ultimate responsibility held by legislatures, and may be of several types:

1. commercially competitive corporations which redistribute income and power (e.g., Potash Corporation);
2. non-competitive, monopolistic corporations (e.g., Hydro);

3. agencies (e.g., liquor distribution, regulatory bodies).

Federal-Provincial Relations
The concept and process of decentralization should extend to provincial and municipal governments. However, impulses toward decentralization must take account of the obvious need for central institutions within Canadian federalism.

THE ISSUE
The Political Process

The apparatus of the state and the nature of the government's mandate is inappropriate and requires reform.

DISCUSSION

Government and the Public
The relationship between government and the public cannot be solved by an increased use of referenda, which may curtail the rights of minorities. Some form of proportional representation may be appropriate. Different social and economic groups should be represented in the Legislature. This kind of political system would be more open, fluid and responsive.

Recall is an inappropriate instrument because it would tend to eliminate members' ability to do what they think is right or to lead public opinion.

Government and the Party
Relations between elected social democratic governments and social democratic parties should be improved through better internal communications, education programs, and involvement of the party in cabinet decision-making. Better

communication with government and access to avenues of power should be extended to all citizens through the creation of economic and social planning councils with representation from government, business and labour, leading to a form of extended tripartism.

Government and Caucus
Cabinet should be elected by caucus (cf. Austrian system) and the committee system should be enhanced to allow more backbench and caucus input. A *bona fide* caucus committee would work directly with ministers and parliamentary secretaries. This would open up the political process to more democratic control.

Electoral Reform
Government advocacy advertising should be regulated, similar to the control exercised over election financing, and should be prohibited during election campaigns. All polling financed by public funds must be made public. Advocacy advertising by private corporations should not be tax deductible. All committees of the legislature should establish annual spending limits. A fixed four-year term at both federal and provincial levels is desirable, with the obvious proviso that the term of a defeated government would be cut short.

Control of Bureaucracy
Application of the principle that policy precedes and controls the state apparatus would do much to create more accountable government bureaucracies.

Redistribution of Power
Decentralization
Diffusion
Devolution

A Guaranteed Annual Income is a more efficient form of reallocating existing resources than are multiple, separate welfare programs. It would ensure less paternalism and grant people more control over their lives.

Devolution of power, worker control and co-operatives are generally worthwhile goals, but they carry some contradictions and problems which demand a case-by-case approach. One tactic would be to sell Crown corporations to worker co-ops and communities, with government assuming the role of coordination.

IV
THE WORLD

DEMOCRATIC SOCIALISM IN A HOSTILE WORLD*

Clay Perry
Legislative Representative
Western Canadian Region
international Woodworkers of America

WE HAVE COME UPON EVIL TIMES. Evil not only in the sense that the international establishment imposes anti-human decisions, but also in the more disturbing sense that much of the public has ceased to believe that there are alternatives to these anti-human decisions. This is not surprising, because the public is not being presented with alternatives.

In Canada, real unemployment runs between 15 and 20 percent; the cost of unemployment rose from 1.8 percent of Gross National Product in 1967 to 12.3 percent in 1981. A massive and backward monetarist transfer of wealth and power from the relatively, and often absolutely, poor to the relatively, and often absolutely, rich, caused an *increase* of about three billion dollars annually in interest payments.

* Mr. Perry's paper "Democratic Socialism in a Hostile World" was read to a discussion group focusing on The World. An abridged version appears here. The complete paper is available from the Boag Foundation.

(Eighty billion in Organization for Economic Co-operation and Development [OECD] countries.) Eighty economists, including two former federal Finance Ministers, signed a public appeal for a shift away from "the debilitating role that monetary policy has played." The left is unable even to introduce alternatives into the general political dialogue. This unprecedented, staggering shift of power has not been subject to any kind of effective examination.

The most massive monetarist transfers took place in 1982, but U.S. net interest in 1981 was already at 7.4 percent of GNP, double that of a decade earlier. At the international level, debt servicing for 21 major borrowing countries (i.e., undeveloped, relatively poor) increased from about 37 percent of their export earnings in 1975 to about 80 percent in 1982. Interest payments from the Third World to the U.S. were, at peak, up $60 billion annually. *Fortune* estimated that around January, 1983, the net transfer of funds, including principal amounts loaned by developed countries, would be from the poor to the rich.

What are the implications of this massive transfer? These are not amounts with which people buy groceries or sawmills, but amounts with which whole industries are shifted from continent to continent, armies maintained and whole areas of research and technologies monopolized. How do we fix public attention, or even the attention of committed social democrats, on this giant and foreboding phenomenon?

The International Monetary Fund [IMF], which together with the World Bank, acts as enforcer for international capital, insists as a condition of urgently required loan refinancing, that Brazil "open" its computer market to "world" (i.e., U.S. and Japan) suppliers. Although socialists may not be quick to sympathize with Brazil, this is a case in which a developing country, correctly diagnosing the relationship between the development of new technologies generally, and of computers specifically, reacted to protect an infant industry. The IMF insists that any changes in trade patterns, which imply changes in the world distribution of labour, are to be on their terms. The IMF did not object to immense military and quasi-military outlays, though there is no doubt which created the greater drain on the Brazilian economy. Loans to El Salvador from the U.S., the IMF-World Bank and other western sources more than doubled from January, 1980, to January, 1983, while loans to Nicaragua from the same sources during the same period were cut in half.

A super-government, endorsed by the Trilateral Commission and free from the vagaries of electorates, is very rapidly being exported around the world. Its present jurisdictional power lies within debtor countries, especially those forced to negotiate refinancing. But as industries are increasingly located in the so-called Third World and Export Processing Zones [EPZs], and as unemployment in OECD countries endures, the leverage will lengthen and extend. We will see an increase in the Fellini-like irony of politically active voters seething over neglected potholes in their lanes but growing resigned to soaring interest rates on their mortgages and to the possibility of their workplace being shut down in favour of Alabama or Brazilian operations.

Liberal and democratic socialist forces must contend, also, with the problem of runaway capital. In Canada and the United States the unstated assumption is that corporations have an inviolable right to move their capital around the world in search of ever cheaper, more docile labour, more supine tax regimes and more forgiving environmental standards.

The most extreme version of this phenomenon is the Export Processing Zone. In 1982, more than 50 countries had developed EPZs or were planning to. According to the United Nations Industrial Development Organization [UNIDO], in developing countries in 1980 there were some 52 zones engaged primarily in manufacturing for export. Twenty of these were in Asia; twenty in the Caribbean and Latin America. Some 30 zones are under development. EPZs are also found in market-oriented and centrally planned industrialized countries.

UNIDO estimates the net addition to foreign investment by EPZs in developing countries at $10-15 billion U.S., based on a net addition to employment of one million persons and an investment-employee ratio of $10 U.S. to 15,000.

The policy package being promoted by the World Bank includes inducements for exports and reduction of tariffs on imports. In the 1960s, developing countries adopted laws and systems which gave incentives to foreign investment, particularly to ventures which produce for export, and assumed that further development would come through the "trickle down" mechanism. "Trickle-down" is the theory that if the birds are starving, you should feed the horses more and better grain.

Since the mid-1970s over one million jobs have moved from North America to EPZs in various parts of the world, chiefly Asia. Wages, listed in advertisements bought and paid for by countries such as Malaysia, Thailand, Mauritius and Colombia, are between $1.50 and $2.10 U.S. per day.

Of course, wages do not tell the whole story. The work is generally conducted in isolated, almost slave-camp conditions. The average working life in electronics assembly is four years, following which the workers return to their villages with what remains of their vision. Unmarried women between seventeen and 23 years of age make up 90 percent of the assembly work force in the electronics industry. A whole battery of methods is used to manipulate and control the women. Publications extol traditional female attributes, and recreational activities such as beauty contests are promoted.

The enterprises are established primarily by North American corporations. Many of us participate in pension plans that support these enterprises. They are not integrated with regional economies. The workers cannot save, the products can be purchased only by the wealthiest of nations, no important materials are purchased from the countries concerned, no tax revenue is realized.

The Canadian version enunciated by Ottawa is only slightly less blatant.

> Canadian workers have to be competitive with those of the U.S. and Japan. If they are so obdurate as to refuse, we will introduce wage controls and impose competitiveness upon them.

Victoria is less subtle. Section 3 of B.C. *Technology Assist-*

ance Act states that the "Labour Code does not apply to certain employees":

> [The] Minister may, on the recommendation of the trustees of the foundation, order that any employer who carries on a business of a type described in the Schedule is exempt from the provision of the Labour Code, R.S.B.C. 1979, c. 212 and where the Lieutenant Governor in Council makes such an order, the Labour Code does not apply to that employer or any of his employees.

The message is clear. If we can find workers anywhere in the world, delivered to us more cheaply, willing to work in more dangerous circumstances, made by any means more servile, we will have Canadian workers match those circumstances, either voluntarily, by legislation, or with the connivance of the IMF-World Bank. This reintroduces the old problem of international labour solidarity.

The strategy has been employed by the current government in British Columbia: find a buzz-word with generally favourable connotations, in B.C.'s case "restraint," in the international case "free trade," introduce a package of measures, however large and however unrelated to the former meaning of the buzz-word, labelled with that buzz-word. The strategists of the right need not concern themselves with the possibility that the commercially controlled media will expose or examine this tactic. In British Columbia, the government introduced measures to cripple human rights enforcement, to deprive renters of any avenue to appeal rent increases or eviction, to make a huge shift in private sector negotiating power from employee to employer, and the commercial media dutifully, obsequiously, referred to them all as "restraint."

Countries like the U.S. and Canada that have opted for these policies have suffered more than those that have resisted. Canada dropped from second to eleventh in per capita income from 1960 to 1980, and our position has slipped further since then.

Although comparative statistics tell a woeful tale, Henry Steele Commager's questions are more memorable:

> . . . how did we get from Independence Hall to Watergate, from Yorktown to Vietnam, from Washington to Nixon? How did we get from Franklin's order to the American navy not to attack Captain Cook as he was engaged in work beneficial to mankind, to the vote in Congress banning the use of any American money for the relief of North Vietnamese children by the United Nations? How did we get from Tom Paine's proud boast: "But where is the King of America?. . . Know that in America the law is King," to the official lawlessness of our own time? How did we get from Jefferson's great assertion of faith in his First Inaugural Address–"If there be any among us who would wish to destroy this union, or to change its republican form, let them stand undisturbed as monuments of the safety with which error of opinion can be tolerated where reason is left free to combat it,"–to the use of surveillance, wiretapping, security checks, censorship, and agents provocateurs? How did we get from The Federalist Papers to the White House Transcripts? And how did we get from an unquestioning acceptance of the axiom that eternal vigilance is the price of liberty to the kind of petulant boredom we display towards revelations of duplicity, mendacity, corruption, and turpitude without parallel in our history?

How did *we* get from "right to work," meaning, as it did in a 1943 League of Nations publication:

> . . . that governments are responsible for avoiding large-scale or protracted unemployment and furthermore, that no head of family. . . or single person should be kept for long periods of time in enforced idleness when he is able and willing to work.

to meaning what it does today, effectively a law against collective action?

How did we get from "free trade," meaning:

> . . . that the benefits of modern methods of production are made available to all peoples both by the progressive removal of obstructions to trade and by courageous international measures of reconstruction and development.

to its present meaning:

> a stratagem with which international capital can undermine, not just the terms and conditions of collective agreements, but the fundamental human values cherished by western civilization.

The answers, like the problems, have to be international in scope. During the postwar expansion period social democratic parties deluded themselves by believing that if they moved just one more increment to the right, dropped just one more nasty word–like "nationalization"–from their lexicon, they might meekly inherit the earth. But the same lurch to the right has taken place in Britain, where the Labour Party, at least during the past few years, has returned to doctrinal purity. In the U.S., where no structurally left party has existed in electorally substantial numbers since the late 1940s, the lurch to the right has been no worse.

We have to define much more precisely what we believe and answer the tough questions. How do we accumulate capital in a tough economic climate? Capitalism does it by creating a class wealthy enough to set money aside without sacrificing the baby's shoes; communism does it by central planning. We don't like either mechanism, but have not made clear what we do like. The Workers' Funds established recently in Sweden represent one possibility.

Having defined positions, we have to exhibit some willingness to stick by them against inevitable and massive resistance. If the analysis and alternatives are to have any credibility and if they are not to be simply bowled over by the IMF, they will have to demonstrate international coherence. The Canadian Catholic Bishops Commission on Social Affairs is correct when it says that because the price for free world trade is the abandonment of long-cherished standards central to human values, we will have to begin a process of withdrawal from our commitment to "free trade."

If we are to reconstruct our society, we must first get hold of our society, and repatriate our economy not only in the ways obvious to Canada but within an international context. Do we honestly believe that in paying the internationally determined price for coffee or for calculators made by Texas Instruments, we do *any* worker, at home or abroad, a favour? If so, more of us should read the International Labour Organization's [ILO] report on the circumstances of workers. Goods are produced in EPZs in virtual quarantine from the indigenous society and in conditions of Malthusian poverty.

There is another lead to be taken from the Canadian Bishops. Running parallel to every economic question about maximizing GNP, there are several profoundly important political or moral questions. What does a chosen device or policy mean for the distribution of wealth and power? What does it mean for the quality of human life? What implications does that distribution of wealth and power have for those who cherish a hope for democracy?

During the postwar period of expansion it was difficult to pose hard choices. When economies are experiencing 5 or 6 percent real growth and employers are comfortable enough to extend workers' rights and benefits, however mildly, it is not easy to force a complacent electorate to make tough choices. But the times are now vastly different. If capitalism is not going through a full-scale Marxist crisis, it is going through a sufficiently reasonable facsimile to provide socialists the opportunity to enter the field with the intellectual and moral vigour of old.

The role of unions in social democracy is another matter for analysis. This question would have been harder to raise before Premier Bennett's "restraint budget" precipitated a dramatic demonstration that in an industrial society organized labour is the last repository of resistance. But there is more potential to unions than that. They have organizational links across roughly the same territory as the IMF. They have large pension funds. They have the capacity to *do* the things without first winning general elections. They have the potential of expanding collective bargaining agendas to include flows of investment.

I do not believe myself guilty of naive syndicalism when I suggest that democratic socialism was naive to rely on a system in which virtually all rights were accorded to people *qua* citizens, virtually none to people *qua* workers. It was a curious position, historically, for democratic socialism to take. It is indeed curious that we propose to ensure democracy by reliance upon sixteenth and seventeenth century pre-industrialist institutions alone. It is as though, in an excess of anti-Marxism, we declared the distinction between workers and owners to be irrelevant.

Finally, we must disabuse ourselves of the silly and suicidal notion that to the most difficult problem there exists some 25-words-or-less solution. Solutions to these problems will not be banal. The challenges are difficult, complex, profound. They require dedication and resolution. They also require an abundance of moral and intellectual energy.

DISCUSSION

NEW VOICE: Recently, Donald Regan, Ronald Reagan's treasury secretary, said: "The problem with much of our thinking [meaning those on the right] is that everybody is trying to export more and import less and somewhere the system breaks down." Indeed, there has been a real breakdown in the success of several EPZs because of the effort by some countries to beggar their immediate neighbours or the people one notch down the ladder from them. Singapore is an example. All of the decisions about this process are made at an international level in a corporate sphere. The degree to which transnational trade union relations can be an appropriate competitor to that authority is questionable. Most of the decisions that we have any grasp on are taken at the national level or, as in Canadian circumstances, at the provincial or even municipal level. There is a fundamental imbalance in the relationship which we have not addressed very honestly. Presently, political parties, social democratic or otherwise, are not strong enough to challenge the transnational corporations; indeed, many nation states are not that powerful. The power of transnational corporations is accelerating rather than diminishing.

NEW VOICE: Speaking from an Albertan perspective, which may be somewhat parochial, the fundamental necessity is to decouple our petroleum and coal sectors and perhaps our agricultural industry from multinational companies. The nature of the organization of the units of economic activity is critical. The institution I work in has some interesting implications as a model. Universities, at least successful ones, are generally self-governing co-operatives of academics. It may be, for all its imperfections, a useful model for other kinds of organizations. There is no doubt that alternatives to multinational corporate organizations are required but the specific kinds of alternatives have not been articulated clearly.

NEW VOICE: Speaking from a less parochial, but perhaps more heretical, perspective, we should concern ourselves with the question of whether social democrats have any role in breaking down the polarization between east and west in the world. Are our interests as people as inimical to those of the Soviets and the Chinese as we thought fifteen years ago? We may have much more in common than we realize. We tend to be very apprehensive of discussing this issue for fear of somehow being tainted.

NEW VOICE: A major reason for the world's current economic distress has been the implementation of monetarist policy to fight an inflation which arose mainly because of oil price shocks. If right wing governments are in power and the same policies are applied, there will be future inflationary shocks in the 80s. This has implications not only for the Third World but for all of us. The general public demands action to fight inflation and the left has lost credibility on this issue. A key requirement is to have some means of dealing with inflation other than through monetarist policies that create mass unemployment. Sweden and Austria have been more successful. Currently the best alternative to monetarism and mass unemployment is some form of Incomes Policy and that is a very controversial subject.

NEW VOICE: There is very little solidarity across boundaries among social democratic or progressive groups. It is beginning to grow but it is not very effective. International union solidarity is, of course, an idea that we have heard before. However, it has not been very successful. Perhaps there are other areas where communication and co-operation could be encouraged.

NEW VOICE: We all see ourselves as British Columbians, as Albertans, Canadians or Americans, and we work and think within that framework. Those who exploit labour cross international boundaries at will, whereas political parties and individuals rarely identify themselves as part of a world community. In view of the nuclear arms build up, the time is rapidly approaching when that myopia may be fatal. We should at least develop the same ability to think globally that the multinationals have.

NEW VOICE: The total failure of all existing mechanisms, both international and bilateral, for meeting basic human needs in developing countries has human, organizational, technological, environmental and political dimensions. We should look at the kind of development that is being pursued in China, that Tanzania attempted, and that Israel has done long since. The creation of greater self-sufficiency and confidence in the developing countries would make military adventures unnecessary. Military intervention is very much a part of the global reality, but it stems from our failure to meet human needs in developing countries. It is quite obvious that all existing mechanisms are either extremely damaging to these countries, as well as to ourselves, or they have totally failed.

TRANSNATIONAL ECONOMY AND SOCIAL DEMOCRACY*

Howard M. Wachtel
Professor of Economics
American University
Washington, D.C.

PUBLIC POLICY IN THE MIDDLE of the twentieth century was constructed on the foundation of Keynesian economic policies and social welfare programs. The one promised us stable economic growth and the other was designed to promote economic security. In the past ten years both of these policy strategies have been in retreat in the face of economic instability, ideological challenge and programatic paralysis. This occurred in all the industrial democracies at some time in the late 1970s and early 1980s–most prominently in Great Britain and the United States but also in Canada and France, and even to some extent in the countries of central and northern Europe.

* Prof. Wachtel's paper "Transnational Economy and Social Democracy" was presented to a discussion group focusing on The World. An abridged version appears here. The complete paper is available from the Boag Foundation.

As these changes have been occurring in the political economy of nation states, the world economy has been wrenched by international monetary instability, undulating commodity prices (particularly for oil and food), economic stagnation, and a realignment of the balance of economic power in the world.

The world economy today is a *transnational economy*, where production and banking transcend the narrow public policy boundaries of the nation state and function outside the traditional rules of international economic relationships among countries. The importance of the impact of a transnational world economy on a shifting political-economic consensus in the industrial democracies has not been given the attention it deserves in proposals for progressive economic strategies. The transnational economy is distinct from the international economy which is governed by public international rules established by nation states. The transnational economy consists of private commerce, finance, and communications that are designed to break down both domestic public regulation and international public rules. Private institutions–multinational corporations and banks–are the key players in this drama, and they have such control over the commanding heights of the world economy that they can transcend public regulatory authority, both domestic and international.

The World Economy and Keynesian Economic Policy
Stable economic growth is more likely to occur in an economic environment of predictability. For the 25 years after World War II, fixed exchange rates, as part of the Bretton Woods system, constrained a key market: money. In retrospect, this system provided a certainty that enabled individual countries to pursue their own national economic strategies more successfully than today, without damaging spillover effects either from other countries or from the international monetary system.

During the Bretton Woods period, between 1948 and 1971, world industrial production grew by a real rate significantly higher than any other recorded throughout the history of the industrial world. The Bretton Woods system formally came to an end between 1971 and 1973. New arrangements deregulated international money markets. This has had a profound effect on the ability of individual nation states to follow their own self-contained economic strategies.

Money and its mystical qualities came to dominate public attention. Monetarism as a social philosophy quickly gained credence where previously it had occupied a small corner of the economics profession. In the corporation, managers of money ascended to key positions, frequently replacing chief executive officers who previously had risen from the production side of the firm.

The intensification of the interconnections within the international economy meant that economic shocks were transmitted more rapidly. Technological changes in global communications enlarged this process. While the private economy became globalized, public policy remained rooted in the nation state. Keynesian economic policies work best when nation states can pursue economic strategies in a closed economy and where centre stage is held by the production of goods and services without intrusion from unpredictable transnational monetary phenomena.

The Transnational Monetary System

Nowhere are changes in the international economic order more apparent than in the international monetary system. Eurodollars are U.S. dollar deposits held by commercial banks in Europe. They circulate in international trade but do not make up part of the United States' domestic money supply unless they are repatriated. At the beginning of the 1970s, toward the end of the Bretton Woods system, Eurodollar credits were just under $100 billion. By the end of the decade, Eurodollar credits had grown more than ten times to over one trillion dollars. * Ironically, the Bretton Woods system of fixed exchange rates organized around the dollar

---

* For an elaboration of these ideas, see Howard M. Wachtel, *The New Gnomes: Multinational Banks in the Third World*, Washington: Transnational Institute, 1977.

came to an end between 1971 and 1973 because of the perception in international financial markets that there was an excess supply of dollars relative to demand.

The rise of OPEC, the second great world economic event of the 70s, gave the dollar a reprieve. With the tenfold increase in the price of crude oil, the demand for dollars grew once again because OPEC countries accepted payment only in dollars. Either the world economy would stagnate if more dollars were not available–causing a liquidity crisis of unimagined consequences–or the size of Eurodollar credits would grow. Some of both happened, but largely the dollar credits were created to support the real volume of oil consumption needed to keep the world economy afloat. The ultimate consequence of the growth of Eurodollar credits, however, was economic stagnation, inflation and world debt under the umbrella of a new transnational monetary order.

The supply of Eurodollar credits grew three times faster than the rate of growth in the real volume of world trade in the 1970s. The root of the problem is an enormous growth of dollar credits that cannot be supported by real economic growth. A sword of Damocles hangs over the world economy and its ramifications for progressive political-economic strategies must be fully comprehended.

The *excess supply* of Eurodollar credits can be managed in the present institutional arrangements in the world economy only by creating *sufficient demand* to stabilize this crucial transnational money market. Demand is created either through direct intervention by central banks or by higher interest rates in the United States than would otherwise be necessary to stabilize domestic money markets.

Throughout the 1970s there were successive runs on the dollar as holders of dollars outside the United States became susceptible to speculative fever whenever a real or perceived crisis arose. Typically, a speculative run against the dollar was controlled, until 1977, by foreign central banks intervening to prop up demand by buying dollars with their own currencies. This policy was inflationary for two reasons. First, the influx of dollars was not insulated and they found their way into the American domestic demand. Secondly, when intervention was necessary, money supplies had to be increased in other countries to provide the hard currency needed to buy the dollars. Therefore, compared to the U.S., rates of inflation were higher in Japan, Europe and Canada because governments had to increase domestic interest rates to dampen the flames of inflation. West Germany was the only OECD country with a lower inflation rate than the U.S. between 1971 and 1979.

Despite the fact that countries do try to intervene in transnational money markets to acquire an advantage in international trade, the transnational monetary order functions essentially without any international public rules. The world economy is paying a heavy price for maintaining an unregulated transnational monetary system. That price is higher interest rates, economic stagnation and the rise of monetarism as a conservative political-economic program. It has put progressive social democrats on the defensive and cast them adrift, seemingly without a coherent platform that is able to capture the heart and imagination of its own natural constituency.

Monetarist Political Economy

The deregulation of international money markets thrust multinational banks into a strategic position in the world economy. The executives of multinational banks have come to dominate private economic affairs while public monetary officials—finance ministers, managers of international monetary institutions and central bankers—control the commanding heights of economic policy, both domestically and internationally.

This narrative would not be complete without a brief mention of the circuit of global monetary affairs in the 1970s. As indicated earlier, the rise of OPEC and its attendant inflation in oil prices was the initial source of the growth in demand for dollar credits in the world economy. The instruments for this expansion were the multinational banks which could expand dollar credits in an unregulated environment by operating transnationally—outside of the regulatory reach of the United States. A small increase in the money supply inside the United States could be magnified without limit in the Eurodollar markets when dollars became payments for oil to an OPEC country and were deposited in bank branches outside of the United States.*

The Gulf states in OPEC acquired surpluses–earnings in excess of their expenditures in the world economy–of about $600 billion between 1973 and 1982. This liquidity was supplied through the Eurodollar markets where the multinational banks could expand their dollar credits without limit since there is no reserve requirement against these deposits.

The transfer of some $600 billion of economic surplus to oil-producing countries from oil-consuming countries had its counterpart in the growth of world debt with financed balance of payment deficits for many of the oil-importing countries. If a country could not earn enough dollars through exports to pay for imports, it either had to deflate its economy or borrow. Countries did some of both but the borrowing of the 1970s plagues us in the 1980s. With about $700 billions in debt in the world, the international monetary system has had to scurry to find ways to rollover, stretch out, and renegotiate the debt. Much of this debt cannot be repaid except in the most unrealistic of economic scenarios–a rate of world economic growth that exceeds any achieved heretofore. Yet the banks cannot find the means to write off these bad debts without precipitating a global financial crisis.

In the past ten years, attention of policy makers, both in the United States and internationally, has been on the sequence of events that has brought us to the possibility of international financial collapse. The surface manifestation is Third World debt that cannot be repaid, an excess supply of Eurodollar credits which requires very high interest rates to keep a finger in the dike, and periodic financial bailouts of the multinational banks through higher taxpayer subscriptions to the International Monetary Fund. Beneath the surface, however, and of more consequence for progressives, is the root cause of this problem, located in the decision to deregulate interna-

---

* For an elaboration of these ideas, see Howard M. Wachtel, "A Decade of International Debt," *Theory and Society*, 1980, pp. 503-518.

tional money markets and the subsequent emergence of a transnational monetary order.

Reconstruction of a progressive political economy, therefore, requires a new form of public management of transnational money markets. Scepticism about "free"markets and deregulation is justified. What has happened in the world economy since deregulation provides a basis for resurrecting the argument for public management of critical economic resources–in this case money. Until unstable monetary conditions come under more control, our ability to influence the contemporary political economy from a progressive perspective will be limited.

Reconstruction of International Political Economy

Three interrelated parts form the whole of a reconstruction of international political economy that would provide a more conducive context for domestic social democratic movements. They are: a return to public international management of foreign exchange rates, equitable arrangements to deal with international debt, and regulation of the global activities of multinational banks.

Management of Foreign Exchange Rates

The purpose of a reconstructed international political economy is to establish a context that will permit countries to follow national economic policies of economic growth, if they choose, without looking over their shoulder at the growth-aborting dimensions of transnational monetary instability. The economic borders need to be figuratively closed by restoring predictability and stability to exchange rates. By shutting off the potentially devastating spillover effects that now exist in a wide open anarchic transnational economy, nations will once again be able to pursue national economic objectives.

Exchange rates should be stabilized among the dollar, the yen and the European Currency Unit within a narrow band. If these large currency blocks can be aligned and stabilized, foreign exchange rate fluctuations will be brought under substantially more control. Technical problems such as the establishment and management of a stabilization fund will have to be worked out, but the techniques for doing this are well known. The stabilization fund should be used to absorb part of the dollar overhang that now plagues the international monetary system. In banking parlance, such arrangements are called "substitution accounts" and their technical dimension is not beyond the reach of human ingenuity.

The stabilization of currency blocks is only an interim measure, however. Full-fledged long-term reconstruction of the international political economy will require some form of Keynes' international currency unit, what he called a Bancor, substantially independent of any individual nation's currency.

The management of the Bancor system is complex and requires international political agreements that seem fanciful in the current atmosphere. By the end of this decade, however, the problems with the international economic system will become more and more destabilizing. Each international economic crisis–whether fueled by debt defaults or a run against the dollar, two sides of the same coin –ratchets up the present system's proclivity towards collapse. These crises are now occurring with more frequency –not just one a year, or one every six months, but now one every three months. Will the nations of the world have the courage and perspicacity to act before we are engulfed by global economic events?

As progressives, we should be out front on this issue because public responsibility in the management of important resources is our natural terrain. International monetary markets are highly concentrated and exempt from many anti-trust regulations, as well as other forms of regulation. The key private bank officials and their counterparts in government and international public agencies routinely meet at the Paris Club, at meetings of the IMF, and with the Bank for International Settlements in Basel. This kind of economic concentration and collusion is never in the public interest. It is time to affirm public rights and responsibilities through the re-establishment of a managed global money market. The global dimension of money in today's high tech communications world is simply too important to be left to the anarchy of the free market with its textbook parable of small entrepreneurs competing in an auction-type market. It just doesn't work that way, no matter what University of Chicago economists say.

Third World Debt

Most of the $700 billion in debt around the world today can never be repaid. These are bad debts and the normal business way of dealing with bad debts is to write them off the books. But the debts are so large and so highly concentrated that any attempt to do this would precipitate a global financial crisis of unimagined proportions. The industrial democracies, therefore, are being held hostage to the imprudence of multinational bankers who have made, and continue to make, whopping profits from this scheme, because taxpayers have been forced to ante-up in order to keep the financial system afloat.

The only way to handle these bad debts is to phase them out gradually. The present ad hoc form of crisis management simply perpetuates the problem. There is a need for comprehensive arrangements among the banks, governments, international agencies and the debtor nations.

Here is the rough outline of such a plan: an international financial intermediary, the "Debtors' Fund," is established. It has the authority to buy the bad paper from the commercial banks and is restricted, in the financing of this operation, to borrowing only on Eurodollar markets. In this way, the Eurodollar overhang is reduced, an essential ingredient for a reconstruction of the international political economy. Third World nations that participate in the refinancing of their debt must concede something too. In this scheme there is no free ride for anyone.

To be eligible for refinancing, Third World nations will have to put up some collateral against their debt. This may take the form of token collateral, such as tangible property owned in the countries that have lent them money (embassy buildings, commercial property and the like) and intangible property (commercial air landing rights, most favoured nation status and other forms of preferential commercial treatment).

Although a mere token, this collateral represents an important symbol of seriousness and responsibility and is a signal to the taxpayers of the industrial democracies that they are not simply being asked to put up new money to replace old money which was improperly used.

The multinational banks, finally, will also have to concede something in return for their part in the global financial bailout that is necessary to keep the international financial system solvent. The banks will have to subject themselves to regulation of their international lending activities.

International Banking Regulations

Commercial banks that operate transnationally outside of their own countries do so largely with impunity from regulation. Any effort to deal with international debt, therefore, requires strict regulation of multinational banking or we will be back in the same situation we find ourselves in today.

The first regulation needed is a reserve requirement against Eurodollars, *higher* than the reserve requirements that presently exist in domestic money markets. The reason reserves should be higher, at first, is the need to reduce as much and as quickly as possible the rate of growth of Eurodollars.

Secondly, the banks must provide more reporting on their international lending activity than they presently do–which is virtually nothing. Reporting will aid regulators in finding the soft spots in a bank's portfolio, will discover any excess concentration of loans to one particular country, and will tell bank regulators whether a particular bank has loaned too much in the international sector.

Thirdly, the interest charged on international loans, now subject only to the flimsiest kind of market regulation, must be subject to public policy influence. Interest rates on international loans have, in effect, had no limit because the borrowing nations have not felt any obligation to repay the loans. They have been willing, therefore, to agree to any rate of interest to get the hard currency, subject only to their ability to maintain a credit rating. The banks, recognizing this, have responded with very high interest charges. When the country defaults, it simply goes to the IMF, which ultimately is funded by the taxpayers, and borrows money to lever a rescheduling from the commercial bank at an even higher rate of interest than before.

The interest game must come to an end, and the way to accomplish this is through the public asserting its right to influence the rate of interest charged on international loans. In these three areas of multinational banking policy, regulatory powers should be deposited with the"Debtors' Fund."

Rebuilding the Social Democratic Agenda

The expansion of the welfare state complemented Keynesian-led economic growth in the 25 years immediately after World War II. A *social accord* was informally adopted in all of the industrial democracies under which labour would comply with corporate industrial policies so long as both the private wage grew and the social wage, represented by social welfare programs, expanded. This period represents the zenith of the welfare state. Since the end of the 1970s and through the 1980s, there has been a conservative attack on the welfare state in all industrial democracies, albeit with varying degrees of intensity.

In all of the industrial democracies, the cultural values of the political and economic systems are in conflict. The political system is organized formally along the principles of perfect *equality:* one person, one vote. The economic system, by way of contrast, is based on *inequality:* one dollar, one vote. Some degree of inequality is accepted in the economic system to provide the private incentives deemed necessary to motivate people to energize the economy.

In Daniel Bell's terminology,* the "cultural contradiction" of capitalism describes the inherent tension between the values of these two systems. Nowhere is this contradiction more apparent than in the international institutions created after World War II. The political institutions enshrined in the

* Daniel Bell, *The Cultural Contradictions of Capitalism,* New York: Basic Books, 1976.

United Nations are based on the principle of one nation, one vote (ignoring for the moment the Security Council). The economic institutions created through the Bretton Woods system are based on the principle of one dollar, one vote.

The economic system cannot function without some degree of inequality. The political system cannot function without a commitment to formal equality. Left to its own devices, the private market system would tend to generate inequalities which the political system could not satisfy without threatening its own legitimacy based on formal voting equality. Social welfare policies are a way for the political system to insert its ideological commitment to formal equality into an economic system bent on sustaining inequalities.

The tension between these two institutions results in pendulum-like swings in the commitment of governments to social welfare policies. Since these policies represent the political system affirming its ideological values over the economic system's values, continuing support depends on factors that render the ideological values of the political system more influential. In the late 1970s and early 1980s, the pendulum swung toward the ideological value structure of the economic system at the same time as the world economy was becoming more of a transnational economy.

The transnational economy, by definition, erodes the importance of the economic role of the nation state, while elevating the influence of the values of the economic system. As the economic functions of the nation state are weakened in this transnational era, the political system cannot advocate its values of equality as effectively as before. The result is a retreat from social democratic policies and an assertion of economic values over political values, a privatization of what have previously been public obligations. Stepping back from the immediate and specific political debates over deregulation and privatization allows us to see that the general political tempo of the times has its roots in the transnationalization of our economies. To regain the initiative in public discourse requires a realization of this fact.

Conclusion

Robert Heilbroner argues that there is an "ill-understood confrontation between political power, which is growing at the national level, and economic power, which is growing at the supranational level." The result, he says, is an "uneasy suspicion that the basic unit of economic policy–the nation state–is not appropriate to the problems of late twentieth-century capitalism."* A reconstruction of international political economy that will permit the industrial democracies to follow their own growth strategies requires a reregulation of global money markets. This sentiment is echoed by Helmut Schmidt, former prime minister of West Germany, and his finance minister, Manfred Lahnstein, when they argued in a perceptive article in *The Economist* that "the self-healing powers of the market cannot take care of all our problems."†

Social democrats can no longer remain on the sidelines while conservative forces are ceded the global economic and monetary terrain. We do so at our own peril. We must throw ourselves into this fray, no matter how alien the language and ideas and no matter how difficult it might be to give up our fiercely held belief that economies function in the context of sovereign nation states. For too long we have stood aside and thrown imperialist brickbats at those who dabble in world economic and monetary affairs. While we have captured the commanding rhetorical heights, our adversaries have monopolized real power in the world economy.

DISCUSSION

NEW VOICE: Where would the money come from to establish and run a debt management institution as a response to Third World debt? If the money is borrowed would we not be back in the same position? At a conference on North-South

---

* Robert Heilbroner, "Economic Prospects," *The New Yorker,* August 19, 1983, pp. 77-78.

†Helmut Schmidt and Manfred Lahnstein, "The World Economy at Stake," *The Economist,* February 26, 1983, p. 19.

relations, a representative of the World Bank estimated the outstanding debts to the private banks as 9 percent and possibly less. Would a debt of that magnitude have such a large effect on the international economy or is it just a scare tactic on the part of the banks to get some countries to pay them back?

WACHTEL: The World Bank and other public agencies always underestimate the problem because they are trying not to frighten people. I would not trust their estimates. The thrust of your question regarding an institution which would buy the bad debts is quite right. It is a mechanism to write off the debts without precipitating a global crisis. During the Great Depression, governments in various countries set up institutions to purchase bad debts and keep things going rather than foreclosing on people's farms and houses. Under the New Deal, the Agricultural Credit Administration bought mortgages from private banks and, instead of foreclosing everywhere, the government kept some people in their homes. Sometimes they collected; sometimes they didn't. At the international level such an agency would provide a telescoping mechanism which would force both parties, the commercial banks and the borrowing countries, to give up something. Everybody has to give up some degree of power, and in the case of the commercial banks, some degree of profits as well.

NEW VOICE: In 1983, the Canadian central bank said they were no longer going to tie interest rates to the money supply. Does that mean that Canada has decided to move away from a monetarist approach? What effects will that have on a basically open economy like ours?

WACHTEL: It might be a signal that you are moving away from strict monetarism. If you want a bilateral arrangement you'd better hitch your horse to the right wagon. It is a risky business. Tying Canadian exchange rates to the American dollar means an overvalued Canadian dollar because the U.S. dollar is overvalued. This will affect trade efforts. Interna-

tional efforts, which are consistent with the social democratic vision of international solidarity, would have more
long-run advantages than any kind of bilateral arrangement.

NEW VOICE: The idea of an international agency to administer bad debts has a familiar sound in Canada, where governments have frequently intervened to bail out companies in
trouble. In the business world when somebody takes over a
bankrupt firm they usually receive partial ownership or at
least some control. I wonder if that is not a real weakness of
your scheme. If debtor countries have made bad decisions
and are basically bankrupt, why should they not surrender
some equity?

WACHTEL: That is a good point. As described, the structure
of an international agency to absorb debt reflects the current
American political context where I have been working with
some members of the Congress and the Senate on these
proposals. This seemed to be the most practical way of gently
nudging us from where we are closer to where we need to be.
These are considered very radical ideas by those very conservative people. Your point is a good one. One might extract, as
a *quid pro quo* in this international collective bargaining
situation, some ownership equity. However, I would not trade
off regulation for equity. Tough and carefully crafted regulation is better than an ownership equity because it is a closed
circuit.

NEW VOICE: Monetary policy, the influence of banks and the
loss of national control over national economics have enormous indirect influence on the lives of ordinary people. They
translate into domestic purchasing and borrowing power and
tie in with a feeling of powerlessness on the part of many
people. With power flowing more and more to international
organizations and banks, how do you reverse the feeling of
powerlessness, the sense that control has moved somehow
far beyond the state, to say nothing of its having been removed
from the provincial or municipal level?

WACHTEL: That is the critical question for social democrats. How do you close the circuit and plug the last leak? How do you control capital?

Nationalization was historically seen as the device. Capital has the ability to go on strike just like labour. Currently we have a massive strike of capital in the world. Capital can strike by moving from one country to another. It can be moved out of real assets into paper assets, which creates a paper world economy in which rates of return can be constructed. There is a massive strike of capital in terms of investment in real tangible productive resources. The last great challenge of social democracies is to develop strategies to deal with the control of capital. It is going to be a long battle. We have not given as much attention to that as we have to things that are solely nation state oriented. I sympathize with the attempt to get political strategies down to the neighbourhood and the community, but we have to deal with the global dimensions in order to effectively enable communities to pursue their own political and economic objectives.

A better understanding of the challenges of the 80s may be derived from looking at history. What happened to the social democratic agenda of the 1890s? The Webbs' argument, elaborated by the Fabians, was to drive wages up through trade unionism. That was to have a salutary effect in that it would drive out the inefficient, low productivity manufacturers and enterprises.

In the 1890s, when Alfred Marshall was constructing neoclassical economics, efficiency was the great catch word, as it still is today. The Webbs were trying to say that socialism could be *more* efficient. Their ideas also reflect a kind of economic Darwinism which was a strand of political economy at the time. The Webbs knew that people would be made residual in the process, that they would become unemployed. They thought that government intervention could counter the unemployment which resulted from a high wage, high productivity, high efficient economy. That agenda remained static until Keynes came along and showed a way in which we could achieve full employment. If you add Keynes to the Webbs–a high-wage economy in the microsector to Keynes in the macrosector–you get a closed circuit. Sweden tried this and did it very well. Stimulating high productivity with high wages, they drove out most labour intensive sectors like textiles. An exception was the lumber industry which remains labour intensive. A very large government sector picked up the unemployment slack. The high-wage/high-growth economy generated high tax receipts which supported social services. It worked well for a while. It was also tried, in a mini-way, in the United States, where it didn't work. John L. Lewis, President of the United Mine Workers, sponsored and supported trade union efforts to drive wages up and automate the mines. He set up The National Bank of Washington using pensions funds and union dues. It didn't work because there was no national full employment policy.

Today there are two problems. First, the ability of capital to go on strike and the inability of government to effectively regulate capital. Secondly, capital is global in its scope while labour is not. Labour prefers to be rooted, not just in a nation state, but locally in community. Although there is tremendous labour mobility all over the world, it is not the first choice of workers. I don't believe that Pakistani workers prefer to go to Kuwait to live and earn their money, rather than stay with their families and associates in Pakistan. Capital is internationally mobile; labour is not. That presents a real dilemma.

What do we do about the problems? As the problems are interrelated, so may be the solutions. Labour's roots in community should be an asset. In the United States there are several hundred billion dollars in union pension funds which could be used for capital development. There are legal restrictions which would have to be removed. However, it has been documented that these funds, in fact, finance the destruction of labour. They finance investments by corporations which shut down plants, automate, and move productive capacity all over the world. The Meidner Plan in Sweden is saying the same thing.

A second argument can be made for increased worker-management and worker-control. The evidence shows that where worker participation increases efficiency, productivity and quality of product go up. Paul Blomberg, an American sociologist, says that hardly a hypothesis in social science is replicated so often. For example, the gentleman on television doing the ads about Remington–"I liked the Remington shaver so much, I bought the company"–is a very interesting entrepreneur. The first thing he did when he bought the company was to close down all foreign plants and pledge to his workers that all production would be done in American plants. Productivity went through the ceiling. The quality of the products went up. He also did away with the executive dining room and executive parking lots. The company has been restored and revived.

The difference between the liberal-progressive reforms of the 60s and 70s and the New Deal period is that during the New Deal the government was seen as the ordinary person's defender, protector and supporter. Rural electrification, agricultural banks and social security supported, defended and sustained families. In the 60s and 70s, for reasons that were not apparent at the time in the United States, a lot of progressive policies threatened neighbourhoods. Busing is a critical example. It is seen as tremendously threatening to neighbourhoods and families. Environmental and safety regulations affected small enterprises which tended to have the worst safety and pollution records and were unable to deal with increased regulation. They didn't have access to capital. They worked more on the margin. They could not pass on the costs of pollution and safety regulation. A lot of those enterprises were community oriented–the old-fashioned kind of small-scale entrepreneur who was not an absentee owner but part of the neighbourhood, there everyday with his sleeves rolled up working like everybody else. This is not an argument against safety or environmental regulations or an argument against integration. It is an argument for finding ways to implement those strategies and objectives which support neighbourhoods, communities and families. In the United States the left has lost that issue. The right, the Republicans, have wrapped themselves in pro-family, pro-neighbourhood, pro-community rhetoric. The left's natural constituency and historical ideology in terms of political and economic solutions can be rehoned to get to the gut instincts of citizens and voters in the political process.

We must utilize pension funds to address the problems of mobilization of capital by establishing a national development bank. As socialists, we should develop policies to restrict the flight of capital. If private capital is not going to invest locally, if it is going to play around with the paper economy, then we must structure policies which ensure investment in real jobs and productive activities that are supportive of communities.

The worker-management position would naturally enhance a socialist position. No worker is going to vote to shut down the plant and build one in Taiwan or Hong Kong. In terms of social policy, as distinct from economic policy, we have to achieve our social policy without threatening the very people who are our constituents.

NEW VOICE: I am not sure about union pension funds in Canada, but my feeling is that a great deal of them are in the hands of provincial and federal governments which tend to use them to support deficit budgets. If what you say is correct, it should be possible to decouple ourselves from the transnational mechanisms. Is that the case?

NEW VOICE: I am on the pension committee of the Canadian Labour Congress. Most of the funds are currently in the hands of insurance and trust companies. However, the constructive use of pension funds is now the policy of the CLC.

As a trade unionist, the high-wage theory is music to my ears. It is gratifying to hear that our excessive wage demands can harmonize with a higher social purpose. However, there are still a few problems to be solved before we get flighty with wage demands. It is also appealing to hear a call for a New Deal, supportive of neighbourhoods and communities. But again, there is a major problem. I spent the last ten years negotiating for workers in steel and mining industries. I am acutely aware of our vulnerability to the mobility of capital. We have to talk about ways to have our economy both open and closed to international movement of trade and investment.

WACHTEL: I would let capital do what it wants, but I would attach costs on the grounds that the state must bear tremendous social costs whenever there are partial or total plant shutdowns. Unemployment and unemployment compensation are automatically triggered. A sufficiently high severance tax on the shutdown of a plant would act as a disincentive. Those taxes should be put into a development fund for the region from which capital has been withdrawn. There are precedents in Europe for plant closing legislation.

NEW VOICE: My first response to your comment about the mobility of capital vs. the immobility of labour, and specifically to the example of the Remington Corporation, was to wonder what happened to the workers in those other plants around the world when their plants were shut down so that American workers could be protected. So many of the solutions to North America's labour and economic problems do not include labour in the Third World. I would like to see labour become more mobile. It is probably true that the worker from Jamaica would be happier at home rather than coming to Canada as a farm worker, as would workers in Africa who travel to South Africa to work in the diamond mines. The solution must be stronger international labour ties that would make global working conditions an issue so labour is not competing with itself. The solution is not to be found in circling domestic wagons without regard to the impact on labour in the rest of the world.

WACHTEL: When I was director of the International Economic Order Project at the Transnational Institute, I was always arguing your position. It strikes a very resonant chord. Until International Labour Organization Fair Labour Standards are applied in countries like the Philippines, South Korea and Taiwan, industrial countries must be obliged to boycott those sources of labour. The argument on the other side points out that in the short run this would deny jobs to Third World workers. Realistically, however, international pressure to move towards the ILO Fair Labour Standards can come only from the industrialized counties.

NEW VOICE: A new agency based on U.S. dollars, the Yen and Eurodollars, which are just another form of U.S. dollars, would have implications for international aid. There are severe problems with international aid because the U.S. political direction controls how aid dollars are used. How would this plan enable us to effectively give aid to the countries which need it?

WACHTEL: It is a large question. The Anusha Initiative–published in *Development Dialogue* by the Dag Hammerskjold Foundation deals with this question.

NEW VOICE: How can we begin to achieve international agreements without necessarily having to involve all countries in that process? That seems to be a political impossibility at this point for obvious ideological reasons. Is there any merit in attempting, amongst social democratic governments or middle to left progressive governments, to institute slightly smaller scale international agreements?

WACHTEL: Certainly, several groupings seem logical. You could have representation by primary commodity producers, representation from newly industrializing countries, regional representation, or representation by economic function in the present economic division of labour.

KEYNES REVISITED*

D. Ruben Bellan
Department of Economics
University of Manitoba
Winnipeg, Manitoba

IN 1939 CANADA'S UNEMPLOYMENT RATE was approximately 20 percent. By 1941, as a consequence of the government's enormous spending on the war effort, we had full employment. Expenditures on bullets, bombs, tanks and fighter aircraft are not uniquely job creating. Jobs can be created by spending on roads, bridges, schools and hospitals or, if we are fortunate enough to have a plenitude of public works, there is no reason not to reduce income tax, especially in lower income categories, to encourage consumer spending and thereby generate jobs in the production of consumer goods.

Governments insist that expansionary fiscal policies increase budget deficits which inevitably fuel inflation and impose intolerable financial burdens on the country. These claims are insupportable. It has been demonstrated that a

* The article "Keynes Revisited" is an edited transcription of Prof. Bellan's presentation to a discussion group focusing on The World.

budget deficit does not necessarily aggravate inflation. The government's deficit in 1983 was bigger than it had ever been and, totally contrary to the thesis presented so vehemently, the inflation rate went down. If governments borrow from within the country, the debt is not a genuine burden. While it is true that the federal government has to pay interest on bonds floated to finance deficits and must raise taxes to get the money to pay that interest, the fact is that the Canadian people own the bonds. The government must go through the rather silly procedure of collecting taxes in order to pay the interest. That financial exercise is a nuisance but it is not genuinely burdensome, as it would be if the money had been borrowed outside of Canada and interest payments had to be made to foreign bond owners.

The arguments which purport to justify government's failure to adopt stimulative economic policies do not hold water. The real reason that we have inflation is not budget deficits but the simple arithmetic fact that for the last fifteen to twenty years the actual output of goods has increased by 2-4 percent a year whereas wages and profits have risen 10-15 percent a year. You don't have to be a professor of economics to realize that if you produce 3 percent more and pay yourself 15 percent more, there will be an increase in costs and prices. In order to deal with the kind of inflation problem that we have been experiencing, we absolutely have to have an Incomes Policy which will ensure that the aggregate increase in wages and profits in the country corresponds to the increase in productivity. Apparatus of control can be designed to be reasonably consistent with the maintenance of a free enterprise economy.

Policy must be developed which is cognizant of historical developments. During the 1930s the Canadian labour force included a very large component of poorly educated people; immigrants, many from peasant stock, came to Canada with very humble aspirations and expectations. Consequently, even though their wages were much lower than those paid to professionals, the workers of the 30s humbly accepted this disparity. That situation has radically changed. The labour force in Canada today is composed almost entirely of well-educated people, in that they have been conditioned to aspire to a middle class standard of living. They are not prepared to accept the gross income disparities which were submissively accepted in the past. There are irresistible historical and social pressures moving us toward a very significant reduction in inequality of income. The inflationary pressure that we have been experiencing reflects in considerable measure this historic pressure for the reduction of inequality. It is imperative that the arrangements that we make to deal with inflation accept the fact that incomes must be more equitably distributed.

The procedure of paying people on the basis of time sufficed during the 1930s when the typical worker was terrified of losing his job and hence did his very best to make sure his employer had no cause to fire him. He did not consider asking for a raise for that certainly would be cause for firing. Workers were as productive as they could possibly be out of terror. This too has radically changed. Workers are not nearly as terrified of losing their jobs. They feel very strongly that they are entitled to higher pay, they are organized into strong trade unions which have the economic muscle to lever increases in pay. Ultimately, there must be a change in worker-management relationships and particularly in the type of pay accorded to workers. The worker of the 1930s was often just an extension of a machine. Now workers are well-educated, knowledgeable and have significant self-confidence. Using their dollars, their initiatives and their intelligence, they can make a different type of contribution to production. That contribution must be rewarded not simply by fixed hours of paid work but according to productivity. The optimal way of achieving that would be some sort of profit and ownership sharing which would encourage in the worker an owner's regard for the enterprise.

DISCUSSION

NEW VOICE: The last Labour government in Britain began wide-ranging discussions on Incomes Policy based on the view that trade unions would not accept a wage policy. Once you take the lid off the question of who gets paid what for doing what, you can't put it back on again. The idea of parallel differentials is absolutely right. Service sectors present great difficulties in terms of bringing profit sharing and worker ownership into the system. Although it is necessary to increase worker ownership and control over capital, there are services which cannot be measured in terms of productivity and where attempts to increase productivity generally result in reducing the number of people delivering the service. One doctor looks after 5,000 people instead of 2,000

BELLAN: I agree. There would be difficulties. However, we ought to institute profit sharing arrangements as persuasively as possible even though there are areas where they may not apply. If some form of profit sharing were implemented where practical, the market would tend to produce relative equality of income in the service sector.

NEW VOICE: Your job creation emphasis was largely on the consumer, as opposed to the conserver, society. What are the main areas in which you see realistic job creation over the next ten or twenty years in Canada?

BELLAN: There are enormous possibilities for job creation in public works which are compatible with the philosophy of the conserver society. Beyond such traditional projects as resurfacing roads, public works projects can address environmental concerns. Many of our sewage disposal arrangements are inadequate. You can't swim in Lake Ontario and Toronto's beaches are unusable. Infrastructure improvement need not be incompatible with conserver society ethics.

NEW VOICE: I have two questions. If productive output is tied to equitable distribution, what happens when the Gross National Product actually goes down? Secondly, how do we deal with the very large portion of the labour force—specifically women working in the home and those engaged in volunteer services which contribute to the social structure

–which is neither in wage labour nor the service sector and would not benefit directly from profit sharing mechanisms?

BELLAN: Real consumption can never exceed real production. If we produce fewer goods, then we must consume fewer goods. Full employment would go a long way to ensuring increasing productivity. Women who work at home are supported by men who work in the market and their incomes will reflect the incomes of the persons upon whom they depend. Where individuals, such as the elderly and the handicapped, are not supported by an income worker, then the issue becomes a question of generosity. Those people must be looked after.

NEW VOICE: The left holds onto two myths in its economic thinking. One, that it will be possible to constrain the movement of capital. The notion that we can erect a phalanx of money walls at the national borders remains–to my amusement, embarrassment and discouragement–the firm conviction of the British Labour Party. Two, that it will be as possible to control profits as it is to control wages. The experience in Canada, and the experience of every other democratic country which has instituted an Incomes Policy, is that you cannot control profits and the repatriation of capital as successfully as you can control wages. There is no evidence that control mechanisms have been developed which work.

THE CONSCIOUS SPIRIT OF RESISTANCE*

Patricia McDermott
Labour Lawyer
Sociologist
Toronto, Ontario

WE ARE IN THE MIDST of an economic transformation often termed the "Second Industrial Revolution." This transformation, which involves the merging of microelectronic and telecommunications technologies, is well on the way to pushing computing power into every conceivable area of work. The major players are large transnational corporations, which are not only the major producers of the new equipment, but the main purchasers as well. Some aspects of computerization are proving harmful to working people. Any strategy which attempts to reverse or slow these trends must necessarily deal

* The article "The Conscious Spirit of Resistance" is an edited transcription of Ms. McDermott's presentation to the discussion group which focused on The World. The ideas presented here are elaborated upon in her paper "Microtechnology, Work and Neo-Luddism," which is available from the Boag Foundation.

with the corporations either directly or through government agencies. Given the weakness that nation states, particularly Canada, have demonstrated in their dealings with global firms, this will not be an easy task.

The two main problem areas repeatedly stressed by those concerned about the impact of the new technology on work are displacement/unemployment and the closely related problem of deskilled/degraded work.

Displacement

The changing nature of work and displacement are related. Today technological displacement means unemployment. Researchers are unable to prove the extent to which technological change is responsible for unemployment, although many economists are beginning to analyse the situation in those terms. The auto industry provides a good example. In North America, 300,000 auto workers have been laid off, not because of local technological displacement, but because of the erosion of the domestic U.S. market by the Japanese. The technological displacement occurred in Japan. The Japanese are able to deliver cars to the North American market highly competitively, partially because they have adopted the new technology. The relationship between layoffs and technology is demonstrated by the fact that U.S. auto manufacturers are rapidly retooling to automated robotic plants.

Attrition is another major way that companies are cutting back on the size of their labour force. Canadian banks are automating rapidly. Hiring levels are constant or declining. As consumers, you participate in this strategy. Consumers provide the labour component when they use automatic equipment. In New York's City Bank, 50 automatic tellers are supervised by one human worker. The Toronto Dominion and the Bank of Ontario are planning automation.

As it becomes more evident that technological change creates displacement, the promise that high tech industry will create jobs is touted more frequently. Unfortunately, the promise appears to be false. Articles in *Business Week* and *Fortune* expose tales of U.S. cities which lured high tech firms in the hope of stimulating the local economy. The strategy has not worked. High tech is capital intensive not labour intensive, and the part of the production process which remains labour intensive is being automated. As well as being extremely amenable to automation, chip assembly and wafer dipping are low-skilled, poorly paid jobs, primarily because they compete with Third World operations. Even in the areas where jobs are being generated, the trend is to robotics. Computer programmers and systems analysts are being replaced by canned and pre-packaged programs. Once an automated system with self-debugging programs is operating, few human programmers are needed. Although many computer scientists still cling to the belief that their sanctum will expand, their predictions are more and more being called into question. Philip Kraft in his book *Programming and Managers* predicts that programmers' jobs will decline and be deskilled.

The Allman Commission in Canada and various government reports from Europe predict minor job creation from high tech. The Canadian government has predicted that approximately 50,000 jobs will be created. In Ontario, the 1981 Chisholm Commission forecast that only 14,000 professional and technical jobs would be created in the microelectronics industry in the province by 1985. Obviously, high technology is not going to solve the present unemployment problem.

One of the most confusing aspects of the technology and unemployment debate is the predicted expansion of the so-called "service economy," coupled with the fact that many studies suggest that the service sector will be hardest hit by microtechnology and consequent displacements. This contradiction likely arises because forecasts of growth for service work have been based on past trends that do not take into account the impact of labour–saving computerized equipment. For example, in early 1983 the U.S. Bureau of Labor Statistics predicted that one of the few job categories that would grow by 50 percent in the next decade is "food service worker." Surely this estimate does not take into account the rapid push by fast food corporations to develop technology that will mix, pour and cap soft drinks automatically, not to mention computerized frying baskets and automated hamburger assembly. The U.S. Bureau of Labor Statistics is projecting from the past into the future without considering the real nature of the new technology.

The current talk of "information workers" as a job category that will absorb those displaced from other areas is simply too vague to be taken seriously. Even if one could figure out what these people would be doing, such projections are undoubtedly founded on speculation that does not include displacements from banking, retail, library, sales, telephone and clerical work in the calculation.

It is important to note that most women work in the service sector and that displacement from this type of work presents a serious barrier to the goal of equality for women. The labour market is highly sex segregated. Women cannot easily move into service jobs not typically seen as "women's work." Further, their ability to move to other sectors is highly restricted. The threat of women losing the right to engage in wage labour is an urgent issue that must be addressed in the debate over the new technology.

Although traditional economists maintain that ultimately technological innovation creates jobs, some have become concerned that the transition to a "restructured," "sunrise" economy may be accompanied by staggering rates of unemployment. The relatively new concept of "jobless growth" has begun to gain acceptance in Canada and Europe. Most forecasts are for continued high rates of unemployment throughout the 80s.

Degraded and Deskilled Work
The concept of deskilling of work, and its relationship to displacement and technological change is perhaps best discussed by Harry Braverman in his book *Labor and Monopoly Capital*. Deskilling transfers control of the productive process from the person doing the work to management. Typically, deskilled work is fragmented into a series of simple components which can be done by a less skilled, lower-paid worker, and may, in some cases, become completely automated.

Deskilled work is characteristically boring and monotonous. It is also more vulnerable to monitoring. The workplace is being invaded by computer equipment that counts the keystrokes a data entry clerk makes per second, the number of items each cashier scans a minute, how many customers a bank teller processes in an hour, and the number of bolts an assembly line worker tightens as products pass the work station. With tight monitoring comes inevitable pressure to speed up production. The list of monitoring and speed up campaigns directly linked to the new technology is long and represents a tremendous ongoing battle for unions.

One potential method for combatting degraded work is to bargain for changes within the context of a unionized workplace. Even in an organized context this task will not be easy since technological change has always been considered a management right. Some unions, like the postal workers [CUPW], have a long history of tackling the issue of tech change at the bargaining table. The communications workers [CWC], air line reservation clerks [CALEA and BRAC] and numerous clerical unions have begun to fill in the holes in their tech change contract language. The process is slow and costly. Many unionists feel that the collective agreement route amounts to "too little protection, too late." To make headway on such issues as preserving work skills, health problems associated with prolonged Video Display Terminal use, and detailed electronic monitoring, the nature of work must become a social issue rather than one relegated to the bargaining table.

The solution most often suggested to counter technological unemployment is retraining. Unfortunately, as has become clear, the next question is: retraining for what? The tragically high unemployment rates for those under 25 reveal the urgency of finding solutions for the training dilemma. Although programs which assist corporations to retrain workers for specific jobs should be encouraged, corporate training should not become a sole option for a young person trying to avoid the world of unemployment. The value of a solid liberal arts education is something that should not be forgotten in the plans to build a socialist society.

Concern with the potential problems of high technology and unemployment is not the exclusive domain of unions and democratic socialists. American ingenuity in the realm of popular ideology has spawned an analysis which identifies an attitude called "Atari-Liberalism." Richard Reich, in his recent book *The Last American Frontier,* begins by stating that America is in a period of de-industrialization characterized by a waste of human labour. This theory buys into high tech as a goal and accepts technological displacement and unemployment as necessary. Reich points to the failure to restructure old industries as the major problem with the economy. His conclusion is that human capital is being wasted and the solution will be found in a move to high technology. He recommends that the United States take advantage of the fact that even American multinationals have fled the domestic market and put jobs in other countries. Capital flight and job flight are seen as problems which can be turned to the advantage of the United States. The relocation of jobs in the Third World can provide markets for American consumer goods because people in the Third World are now employed and therefore have disposable income. Reich also says that there will be a long, hard, tough row to hoe and everyone will have to suffer. Democratic socialists should look at the role which Reich outlines for the various actors on the long hard road.

> An industrial transformation on this scale will necessitate close cooperation among business, government and labour. Government must contribute public funds to the massive task of retooling and retraining. In return, business must in fact retool and retrain instead of merely shifting its production abroad in exchange for paper assets at home. And in return for retraining and job security, labour must abandon its rigid job classification, work rules, and cost-of-living increases. This agreement must be extended to other citizens as well, especially the poor, minorities and the young on whom the burden of fighting inflation has fallen

the hardest in recent years. In exchange for fiscal
and monetary policies designed to foster full
employment and education and training programs
designed to give them job-related skills, these
groups must agree to certain cuts in welfare and
other entitlement programs. In short the nature of
the bargain is this: the burdens of economic change
should not fall disproportionately on anyone and
the benefits should be spread broadly and equitably.
In return for this assurance, none should seek to
block economic change.

The fundamental position of "Atari Liberals" is misleading.
When labour sits down at the table now they come from a
position of retreat; they negotiate from a position of declining
power. In that kind of scenario the multinational has not
given up any power. This analysis focuses on the U.S. nexus
and its competitive position relative to Japan and Europe.
Essentially it asks labour and working people in North
America to enter the capitalist scenario of competition which
takes workers right back to the beginning of the industrial
revolution. Traditionally, socialists have responded positively
to the advent of technological change. For over 150 years we
accepted technological change because we believed it would
benefit the commomweal. Perhaps now it is time to say "no,"
to demand that technological change not put ordinary working people in increasingly disadvantaged positions.

To continue to buy into capitalist solutions is to invite a
two-class system. The proletariat and the captains of industry
are being transformed into techno-peasants and technocrats.
We cannot wait until the system is in place and then, as
socialists, take it over. Rather than reading Robert Reich, we
should urge policy makers to read Barry Bluestone and
Bennet Harrison's *The Deindustrialization of America* and
Samuel Bowles' *et al. Beyond the Waste Land.* Democratic
socialists may find truly creative solutions to our problems,
beyond the traditional remedies of legislation, in three
brilliant articles by David Noble in *Democracy* (spring,
summer and fall, 1983) which go through the history of the

Luddites. We have to encounter and bring the spirit of the labour past into the present.

The Luddites were organized bands of workers who in early nineteenth century England, as the popular version goes, smashed machinery out of an irrational fear of change. MIT's David Noble maintains that the Luddites were the last workers to perceive technology in the present tense. In a time of severe economic recession, high unemployment and rising food prices, the workers took direct action, at the point of production, against those responsible for their grievances. British historian E.P. Thompson noted that Luddism was a revolt of the people and not merely the action of a handful of disgruntled workers. The Luddites had unsuccessfully petitioned parliament for reforms to protect workers and turned in frustration to sabotage. Anti-Combination Acts had forced labour organizations underground and it was within these groups that Luddism grew. The massive revolt of the people which Luddism represented, a revolt that could only be contained by extreme repression, was part of the reason for the eventual legalization of trade unions.

The story of the Luddites is heroic and colourful. It is a part of the history of working people that has been maligned. What was, in the context of the period, a rational and, in many ways, successful response to the uncompromising forces of capital should not be portrayed as the actions of "the lunatic fringe." We should restore the Luddites to their proper place in history.

To propose neo-Luddism as one way to intervene in technological change in a cultural milieu where the concept has been so denigrated is taking the risk of appearing irresponsible. It is a risk worth taking. Neo-Luddism is not a program for damaging equipment – it is the conscious spirit of resistance.

We must start handling technology in the here and now. The labour movement is straining with this burden. Unions can't do it alone. Their memberships are skrinking, their funds are in trouble. It has to be taken up by individual workers, consumers and socialist parties. In the face of a huge ideological push to a future which ignores the present, we must bring conflict back to the point of production. We must reject economic determinism in which the present is merely a theoretical position. The present must be more than past consequences on the way to future progress.

DISCUSSION

NEW VOICE: As a labour historian I know and appreciate the Luddites, and as the research director for the Steelworkers for the last ten years, I am painfully aware that McDonald's Hamburgers alone employ more people than the whole steel industry in North America. The most fundamentally challenging or undermining things for trade unions to deal with are technological change and capital mobility. They absolutely drain our strength at the bargaining table. We don't have answers. Part of the problem is the international dimension. Multinational corporations are able to deliver a pernicious and pervasive power at the bargaining table.

McDERMOTT: Money to allow union members to meet internationally should be put on the bargaining table. The need for international unionism is well demonstrated in the film *The New Technology with Progress*. The film shows Ford shop stewards from around the world meeting in Europe. The meeting was an incredibly expensive undertaking and, in this instance, the United Auto Workers footed the bill.

Transnational corporate power is very debilitating for unions. Because work can now be shifted globally to break strikes, international contacts and agreements among unions become vital.

NEW VOICE: We have faced technological change since the beginning of the industrial revolution. Previously our tactic was to redistribute the wealth by taxing the yield from those technologies and putting it back into the economy to create the jobs in medicare, education and social services. Why do you feel we can't do that now? If I can get out of the Trail smelter and the lead zinc furnaces, I'm going to get out. Why can't we create jobs that will enhance civilization.

McDERMOTT: What we are seeing now is most correctly called the second industrial revolution. We haven't been through it before. It is universal both geographically and in terms of sector distribution–it's everywhere in the world, in all aspects of working life.

NEW VOICE: Funding cuts in education add to this problem. We won't be trained or educated to deal with the impact of technological change. Canada will become a Third World country.

McDERMOTT: Coupled with cutbacks in medicare and education is a rise in private sector involvement in hospitals and schools. Institutions which don't make money will be privatized and if they can't be privatized they will not get state support. In education the rhetoric says let industry be responsible for retraining. Corporate education vs. universal education is problematic. What kind of education will people get? What is the future for people trained in this way?

NEW VOICE: What is your vision of what work should look like? Presumably there are some unpleasant jobs that we don't necessarily want to preserve. Do we reject high tech? Do we reject the smoke stack jobs? What do we end up with?

McDERMOTT: We will probably end up with reduced or minimal work. We cannot continue with an eight-hour day and it may be hard to adjust to work as a diminished part of our lives. We will have to develop new values, which can be discerned and developed by looking at how unfettered technology is changing working conditions. For example, one potential effect of technological change is invasion of privacy and control by the state. Although the Big Brother scenario is dramatic, and perhaps alarmist, it does not take much imagination to see that the information stored in government computer systems could be used to implement repressive measures which may be deemed necessary to control a society with massive unemployment. The detailed and subtle information that your VISA record contains is frightening. Where you work. Where you eat. What books you buy. When? Where? Who owns that information? VISA has made it available to lawyers for litigation. The privacy issues are of huge proportions. Computerized security systems can monitor and control access to buildings and movement across international borders and, therefore, could be used to decrease personal freedom and mobility. There is a Big Brother mentality in many of the potential applications of the technology. ·

NEW VOICE: Surely we can struggle toward a definition of work which includes work done in the corporate system, as well as work done at home, in the garden, or for the co-operative or the neighbourhood.

We are talking about the contemporary global political economy and sometimes we trap ourselves because we use a model which defines three worlds, the east, the west and the Third World. The model is outmoded. There is one world. Capital goes wherever it wants to. The Ford Motor Company manufactures components all around the world which are assembled into cars in Canada. Coca-Cola goes to the Soviet Union. Pepsi-Cola goes to China. We have to deal with technological change with a global concept.

McDERMOTT: If wage labour is going to be eroded through global technological change, we may have to consider some kind of guaranteed annual income. It is very important to maintain a global perspective when studying alternative solutions to the problems of high technology. The idea that we should encourage exploitative industrialization in the Third World in order to develop markets for our products which will keep "us" on top in a competitive economy is antithetical to socialist ideals. That's a capitalist model.

NEW VOICE: We should not be too pessimistic about the difficulty of keeping high tech development under control. A fruitful comparison can be made with environmental policies. The United Nations Environment Conference in Stockholm in 1972 produced a certain standardization of laws and values to be taken into account in future industrialization. Today, all over the world, there is some form of environmental policy. These standards are effective and influential. During the 60s, the transportation industry planned to build two-million tonne oil tankers. Nobody today is thinking of building a tanker bigger than 200-400 thousand tonnes. The Concorde is another example. During the 60s and early 70s the push was to develop larger, faster planes. In effect the Concorde project has been dropped. Telephone systems and banking systems, while becoming ever more computerized, are also becoming much more sensitive because as they become more complex they become vulnerable. In Holland, unions have negotiated for controls which in fact make it possible for whole telephone systems to be de-activated by trade union action. The implementation of high technology makes society more uncontrollable. We must teach people to have control of the application of high technology. I am not so pessimistic about our capacity to proceed and to achieve some success. Working hours should be shortened. The Dutch Labour Party's role in studying the impact of hours of work and types of work as it related to the de-industrialization of the Netherlands pioneered socialist research in the field. In Holland everyone accepts that in 1986 the standard 35 hour work week will be reduced by 10 percent. By 1990 it will be 30 hours and the debate on the 25 hour week is coming up. International trade unions should take up this issue and should translate it into practical policies.

Historically, technological change has meant displacement. It is quite clear that you can't stop technological development. But why must the price for development be the dismantling of the welfare state? Why can high tech not bring as much progress to welfare and jobs in the collective centre as it brings to the industrial sphere? The answer to this new industrial revolution is to expand the collective social sector of society. That is what I see from the central European experience.

NEW VOICE: We should also address ourselves to developing alternatives to big systems. Two recent books, John Naisbitt's *Mega Trends* and Paul Hockins' *The Next Economy,* claim to discern the development of a new sub-economy below the high technology economy. If one ignores the fact that they are written by political eunuchs, one can glean possibilities for the development and promotion of localized, small-skills technologies, which strengthen the informal economy and promote technologies that are sustainable. High technologies, because they are still based on the system of using non-renewable products on a very large scale, are not sustainable. As socialists we should be looking at what people are actually doing and what they are trying to do. We need to look for technologies that enable people to control the local economy. We are in a hard fight, if we see our task as taking over high technology industries; the promotion of localized small-scale activity is a winnable battle. Naisbitt and Hockins indicate that such activities are starting. We need to find them, help them, promote them and build them into socialist policy.

NEW VOICE: We are aware of the problems that are being created for socialism; problems are also being created for capitalism. Eliminating or reducing the level of work implies that capitalism can survive without consumers. Socialists find themselves talking about guaranteed annual incomes. Twenty years ago Robert Theobald talked about guaranteed consumer spending.

NEW VOICE: As an American, I am both amused and disturbed by the political implications of the move toward high tech in my country. It has caused an interesting political flip-flop. Conservatives in the United States, who have historically opposed central government and supported states' rights and freedom for individuals, have now taken an opposing position. In energy, they support large centralized nuclear power plants. Legislation allows the federal government to override states' objections to disposal of nuclear waste. Conservatives implicitly subjugate the rights of individuals by supporting the accumulation of great amounts of information by police agencies and government on the lives of individuals. Technological change has also caused a flip-flop in terms of the political left which finds itself standing for the right of localities and local governments to veto certain kinds of technological development. The left finds itself standing for decentralized, small-scale energy systems and supporting the rights of the individual against the centralized state.

NEW VOICE: Luddism is a very bad symbol for a very profound, substantive argument. As an approach by workers to the imposition of technological change, Luddism is an object of fun and derision. The Luddites lost badly. Political discussion of the issues of concern to the Luddites was severely hampered by the methods they chose to use. Today, talk of Luddism promotes a nervous reaction because it is perceived as a frivolous and not terribly relevant part of our political tradition. While our response to technological change is an important question, which needs to be named, it should not have to contend with that initial negative reaction.

McDERMOTT: The Luddites were really the first trade unionists and are a very *relevant* part of our political tradition. Luddism led to the Chartists within a few years. It occurred at a time of food shortages and riots. Popular ideology has distorted socialist history by calling Luddism irrational. The Luddites were the last trade unionists to confront technology in the present tense. They were the last people to control and own the tools they worked with. In a period of expanding international markets, technology was introduced to drive down wages, to allow the hiring of untrained apprentices, to produce lower quality goods for the international market because the employers said they had to meet international competition. The parallels are strong.

Luddites were very successful in their attack on technology. Initially they petitioned government with draft legislation which included a scheme to tax all textiles made on a power loom. The monies were to be put in a fund for unemployed people. Luddism in the night was always accompanied by food riots in the day. In two years of Luddism, a thousand pieces of equipment were selectively dismantled. They were effective saboteurs. They formed armies of hundreds of men and undertook raids on mills. It was truly a people's revolt. The law prohibiting the dismantling or breaking of machines, which had provided punishment by deportation, was changed to make the offence one for which capital punishment was applicable. In addition, administering an oath was made an offense for which you could be hung. Luddism was a secret society and fifteen Luddites were hung within a month. The movement ended.

It should also be pointed out that the right raised Luddism as an issue. Xerox Corporation has a management training film called *The Luddite Factor* which shows flashes of high tech office equipment in the background with a menancing crowd looming up and smashing the equipment. The voice-over intones, "Luddism–it certainly is tenacious." This ideology generates and exploits fear. The theme runs though much corporate management literature and is reflected in advertising. An IBM ad includes the copy: "If computers scare you, just imagine how people felt when they first saw the horseless carriage. The promise of the new era implies change, and change can be unsettling at first. That's why IBM feels that right now is the time to talk about the computerized office and the power you will have over it."

What exactly is the promise of the future? We would do well to learn more about the Luddites. I am not advocating smashing the equipment, but we should resist it. We need time to plan alternatives which address the problems of monitoring, control of data, and working conditions. It has been predicted that nearly 40 percent of people in the workforce in North America will be "on screen" by the end of the 80s. The screen is an important symbol.

A POLICY OF COMMON SECURITY*

Joop den Uyl
Former Prime Minister
The Netherlands

> *a man of courage, who speaks to us*
> *as if we were courageous*
> –Lister Sinclair

THE EFFORTS OF DEMOCRATIC SOCIALISTS in Canada are very important for the sake of social democracy in the world today. It cannot be denied that social democracy has suffered severe setbacks in Europe during recent years. Social democratic parties lost their position of government in countries like Norway, Denmark, Britain, Germany, the Benelux countries and in my own country, the Netherlands. More importantly, democratic socialism lost ground in Asian countries like Indonesia, India and Burma, where, during the 50s, Asian

* The article "A Policy of Common Security" is a transcription of Mr. den Uyl's closing address, which was delivered on the last evening of the conference to a public banquet held to honour the memory of Allan Boag.

237

socialism promised to offer a real alternative. In southern African countries, like Tanzania, Zambia, Mozambique and Zimbabwe, democratic socialism is having difficulty maintaining its identity in the face of the increasing influence of the Soviet Union and communism. It would be discouraging if the peoples of Asia and Africa were left with only the gloomy alternatives of communism and capitalism as means of escaping their misery. At the same time, social democracy has gained ground in Latin and Central America and today many hopes are invested in the democratic development in this part of the world.

There are many people working all over the world to achieve more equality for ordinary people. Looking around the world we know that the fate of democratic and socialist solutions depends to a great extent on the influence our principles and policies have in North America–in the United States and in Canada.

It is very important that democratic socialism exist in Canada. The quality of its efforts, its programs and its policies are critical. It must be an important factor in the shaping of the political image of North America.

The essential question is whether democratic socialism can come up with answers for a world stricken by stagnation and mass unemployment, a world suffering from the loss of detente between the superpowers, a world living in fear of an escalation of the nuclear arms race. What should be the response of democratic socialism to the continuing crisis in the world economy and to the assault on the welfare state? How credible, how reliable are democratic socialists in defending their programs? Social democracy in Europe displays a divided image. In Scandinavia and western Europe, where social democracy has been the guiding spirit for years, socialist parties have been forced into opposition. In southern Europe a series of successes in recent years have brought majority socialist governments to France, Greece and Spain, and socialist prime ministers to Portugal and Italy. How do we explain this discrepancy, and can the explanation teach us something about the problems with which European socialism is now confronted and what that may mean for the future?

The decline has to be viewed primarily in conjunction with the economic crisis and with the resistance to the welfare state. In Scandinavia, even before the Second World War, and in western and central Europe afterward, social democracy has been very much associated with the growth of the social welfare state. It was here that the ideals of social security, full employment and a more equal distribution of income, knowledge and power reached their zenith. It is true, in historical terms, that liberals and Christian Democrats made an important contribution to the development of the welfare state but it was the social democrats who were its most persistent defenders. Since 1945, socialism in Europe has been associated with social progress and with the belief that the crisis of unemployment of the 30s must never again raise its ugly head.

As the economic crisis, which became apparent with the 1973 oil crisis, became more pervasive, socialism and the welfare state increasingly became scapegoats in public opinion. In the eyes of our opponents, the principal blame for the economic recession and unemployment lay with the growth of the public sector and the role of the state. Indeed, many supporters of socialist parties, including workers, thought that socialism had not lived up to expectations. This was demonstrated dramatically in Britain in June of 1983 when many unemployed people and workers voted for Mrs. Thatcher. The situation in southern Europe is quite different. In recent decades socialists have been in opposition in France, Spain and Greece. There the right wing parties are associated with the crisis and the economic recession. There they expect socialists to combat the crises of unemployment and inflation. The postwar expectation of socialist parties in northern and western Europe are now true in southern Europe.

What lessons do we learn from this state of affairs? The political opportunities for social democrats in Europe are tied, in the first place, to the degree to which they can succeed in coming up with a reliable and credible response to the economic crisis and to mass unemployment. It is my conviction that social democracy is not only able to do so but, of course, that it is its duty to do so. We must tell the people the truth. There are limits to economic growth. Technological change needs the response of shortened working hours. We should tell our people that prospects for raising the standard of living will be low, even under socialist guidance. The politics of Reagan and Thatcher and all right wing governments will produce some recovery in the market economy. They might create some new employment in a limited number of highly technical industries, but economic growth and recovery in that fashion will be coupled with mass unemployment and growing polarization between those with work and those without work. The socialist alternative means the restoration of limited and selective economic growth, which places the growth of the economies of the developing countries as a priority. It will open the window on the restoration of full employment but only on the basis of a drastic reduction of working hours and a consistent redistribution of work.

This, in many respects, is not a popular program for some of our own supporters. But it is the only one that is based on both solidarity and present world conditions. The basis of a program of this kind is that the essence of the welfare state can be preserved. Everyone has an equal right to work and income. A policy such as this means a difficult struggle to reform international institutions and to create a program of economic recovery which takes real account of the interests of the Third World. Socialism must provide security and certainty when it comes to work and income, just as it will have to ensure security and certainty when it comes to preventing war and eliminating the threats inherent in the arms race.

The nuclear arms race is threatening to escalate. The government of the United States and the government of the Soviet Union must be made to understand that arguments about the exact amount of strength available to one as opposed to the other is no longer the vital issue. The crucial question is whether one adheres to a system and a strategy in which one's opponent is imbued with the greatest possible fear–we call that deterrence–or whether one opts for a strategy in which the potential opponent's fears are allayed as much as possible. The latter does not exclude a certain degree of deterrence, but the primary objective is security, safety and pacification. This concept of common security through a partnership which includes east and west is provided by the Palme Report, from the Commission headed by our Swedish comrade, Olaf Palme. Basically, what the Palme Report says is that there is absolutely no hope of anyone winning a nuclear war. In today's world, security cannot be achieved by confrontation. Safety has to be founded on a concept of mutual survival not on threats of mutual destruction. I do not want to be misunderstood. I do not believe that the deployment of SS-20s by the Soviet Union is not a threat. However, SS-20s are a category of weapons which ought to have been discussed in SALT III because, in such a broad context, the bargaining options were, and are, greater, and there is a chance of a solution being reached. After all, new American developments would then be a topic of debate as well. The endeavour to achieve parity for every category of nuclear weapons should be rejected. Such a piecemeal approach to the nuclear problem produces an arms race at every conceivable level, from battlefield weapons to nuclear loaded satellites holding the world to ransom. The only way to prevent an escalation of the arms race and to ensure that deployment in western Europe would be redundant is to integrate talks on middle-range weapons and to start negotiations on the reduction of strategic atomic weapons. Such negotiations would be conducted against the backdrop of an overall nuclear equilibrium. Imbalances in certain categories would become of subsidiary importance. The distinction between technical, theatre and strategic weapons would be less significant because one would look to see what the arms can do, rather than the label that has been stuck on them. The problem of the British and French nuclear forces would also be solved more readily in that way. Deployment of new middle range weapons in West Germany and Britain and later in Italy will not force the Soviet Union to take a more pliant attitude. The deployment of Cruise and Pershing II missiles has something irrevocable about it for the Soviet Union as well. The Soviets would assume that those arms would constitute a new American threat to which the response must be a counterthreat. The North Atlantic Treaty Organization should exert all possible influence to see that it does not come to this. It is wrong to keep to the schedule for stationing the missiles if not enough time has been allowed for negotiations. All the parties concerned, certainly all the governments of NATO countries, should think and think again before deploying new middle-range missiles. Political action must concentrate on postponing deployment.

We have to make a choice. Either we opt for ever-greater nuclear arsenals with the growing risk of a catastrophe or we opt for the fundamental idea of a policy of common security designed to provide the potential opponent with as much certainty and security as we demand for ourselves.

PARTICIPANTS' REPORT
The World

THE ISSUE
Social Democratic Governments
and East-West Tensions

DISCUSSION

THE PRESENT STATE OF EAST-WEST RELATIONS creates a danger of war
and presents impediments to the development of both blocs.
The most critical problem is, obviously, the threat of nuclear
war. In addition to the prospect of the annihilation of
humanity, the arms race has disastrous economic consequences, fuelling inflation and diverting resources from
domestic social services and aid programs. Both east and west
suffer the consequences of militarization. In the name of
national security both societies endure a lack of political
accountability and the downgrading of human rights, domestically and abroad. Because of the lack of significant east-west
trade, countries find themselves economically and politically
dependent on bloc "allies." Finally, and tragically, the citizens
of both blocs are denied the opportunity to know the
cultures and peoples of the "other side."

243

RECOMMENDATIONS

End the arms race

Socialists should support the Freeze proposal as an interim measure, initially involving only the USA-USSR. As systematic progress is made the Freeze should be expanded to include other countries and conventional weapons. Socialists should challenge the concept of national sovereignty by strengthening the United Nations, the International Labour Organization and disarmament agencies with greater authority and resources. Socialists should halt arms exports and seek conversion of the armaments industry in their own countries. Socialists should provide moral, financial and legal/diplomatic support for civil disobedience against the arms race, on governmental and individual levels.

Demilitarize Societies

Socialists should provide examples to both superpowers, gradually creating an atmosphere of openness by ending military exemption from "freedom of information" legislation. The military should be accountable to the judicial and legislative process. Major defence and external affairs decisions should be the province of legislative, as opposed to executive, arms of government.

End Economic Isolation and Dependency

Socialists should develop balanced trade between east, west and the Third World. As much as politically possible, established trade relations should be immune from disruptions by diplomatic crises. Aid programs should be expanded, with socialist governments spending a minimum of 1 percent of Gross National Product on aid, with preference given to non-NATO, non-Warsaw Pact aligned countries.

Eliminate Cultural and Communication Barriers

Socialists should initiate people-to-people contact in educational, artistic, sports, scientific, political and tourist spheres. Socialists should strengthen the trade union links between east and west, making political as well as syndicalist connections. Finally, socialists should work to make each bloc's media accessible to the other, taking advantage of recent developments in communications technology and working to extend learning of the languages used in either bloc.

THE ISSUE
Transnational Economic Forces

DISCUSSION

Transnational corporations have created an environment in which democratic control is seriously limited. Transnationals are a negative influence on the social and economic conditions of peoples around the world. At present, there are no global political institutions to counterbalance the influence of these key actors in the world economy.

RECOMMENDATIONS

New and Reformed International Institutions
We must find ways to join with other nations, perhaps through organizations like the Socialist International, to frame new international agreements on economic, monetary and trade relationships which assure the fair representation of all nations. Specifically, the Geneva Accord on Trade and Tariff, the International Monetary Fund and the World Bank must be reformed, revitalized and made more equitable and democratic.

The United Nations should have a role in setting minimum standards for capital conduct. Much as the ILO sets minimum standards for labour, the U.N. could determine minimum standards for capital.

Progressive Nations Should Work Collectively
Parties within the Socialist International, for example, could establish a code of economic ethics, and propose sanctions

which like-minded governments could use to implement and enforce minimum standards.

Nation States Should Act Unilaterally

Individual nation states could legislate to establish rules of conduct for transnationals: sanctions which would act as barriers to entry; severance funds or taxes which would act as barriers to exit; provision for "eviction" of transnationals; limitations on entry of transnationals in specific economic sectors; sanctions against the expatriation of assets. Legislation could allow for schemes such as the Meidner proposal which permit equity participation.

Democratize the Process of Planning

The institutional means to make knowledge of issues and political propositions available at the local level must be developed. The public must have more access to government information in all areas, particularly budgets and proposed legislation, to enable informed public consultation and debate. Partisan special interest crisis management should be replaced by a process for policy implementation which allows time for negotiation, compromise and agreement.

THE ISSUE
North-South World Poverty

DISCUSSION

Social democrats should address themselves primarily to the problem of raising the living standards of the 500 million people on this earth who suffer from malnutrition, ill-health and chronic unemployment.

When developed nations in the north address the development problems of the south, economic solidarity and political solidarity must go hand-in-hand. Democratic socialists recognize that great differences may exist between the needs of the people in developing countries and governments' approaches to meeting these needs. In fact, as with the promotion of agri-business at the expense of land reform, many approaches can directly oppose the welfare of the citizens of non-industrialized nations. Support for people, in the form of direct economic aid, must be accompanied by an outspoken rejection of governments that repress those people. Indeed a major difference between democratic socialists and traditional liberals is that, while both may support economic aid to people, only the socialist emphasizes the political shortcomings of repressive governments, as well as the economic needs of the people.

Economic, social and political independence are interconnected. Families, communities and nations should be able to control their own destiny. On an economic level, this acknowledges both the need for self-reliance and the interdependence of people. On a political level, governments should be popularly based, reflecting egalitarian principles and the aspirations of the people. While economic aid to communities can proceed without support of the nation's government, it is clearly preferable to have the government on the side of the people. On the other hand, people living under repressive governments need both direct and appropriate aid from democratic socialists and expressions of political solidarity in their efforts to obtain social justice.

The promotion of interreliance for poor, primarily rural communities is a recommended approach to the problem of world poverty. Access to simple technologies which enable people to work themselves out of poverty and to furnish themselves with adequate food, clothing, shelter and basic community services such as health, water, transport and education puts economic power into the hands of people who are presently powerless.

During the past 25 years it has become clear that economic aid and development organizations have failed in their attempts to promote activity designed to improve the conditions of the poor. Far from promoting self-reliance and independence among poor countries, most aid programs contribute to conditions of increasing economic dependence and indebtedness. Conventional aid and development programs have contributed to the political divisiveness of many developing countries through gross maldistribution of resources, and have made them a cockpit for the military and ideological struggles between east and west. Conventional aid, dominated by northern capital, has also distorted trade patterns between north and south, compelling the south to export raw materials and manufactured goods while neglecting their own internal markets. The promotion of self-reliance in the south would bring about a more fruitful and egalitarian exchange of goods between north and south. Exports should represent a surplus and should not enter the international market at the expense of the poor in exporting countries.

Economic relations between north and south exist in several forms: through the activities primarily of transnational companies and commercial banks; through international agencies such as the IMF, the World Bank and United Nations organizations; through bilateral, government-to-government aid programs; and through a network of non-governmental organizations of many kinds. Non-governmental agencies are clearly the most successful in reaching poor communities and making appropriate technologies available to them.

The commercial banks have made loans to developing countries on a vast scale. These loans are unlikely to be repaid and widespread defaulting could cause the international monetary system to collapse. The IMF and World Bank, representing the interests of the rich countries, are also promoting the introduction of inappropriate technologies in developing countries. Most bilateral aid programs do the same. (There are notable exceptions, such as the Netherlands).

RECOMMENDATIONS

Aid and Development Programs
Social democratic policy should attempt to change the composition and quality of aid and development programs and practices and, in so doing, to build up a partnership between north and south.

Bilateral Aid

Governments should channel bilateral aid funds through non-governmental organizations, particularly those of a social democratic nature, and, in the process, should substitute grants for loans. This is the only way to promote self-generating economic growth without adding to the indebtedness of poor countries.

Appropriate Technology

The question of appropriate technology is central to such a change. The high-cost technologies of the north, based on energy and capital instead of labour, are not relevant to the needs and resources of the poor. The technologies required for self-reliance among communities, both in the north and the south, are generally those that are relatively small, capital-saving, simple and non-violent toward human beings and the environment.

The right of developing countries to establish their own development priorities and to strengthen their ability to choose appropriate technology must be affirmed. Support should be given to those organizations in both rich and poor countries which demonstrate democratic control of appropriate technology development. Social democrats should attempt to ensure that all lenders to poor countries provide details of relevant technological choices. This would apply to banks, transnationals, other international lenders and bilateral programs.

Transnational Fiscal Policies

A special international mechanism designed to lighten the burden of indebtedness of poor countries should be created. This agency should regulate international payments to prevent a recurrence of the current debt crisis and to forestall the growing instability of an international monetary system dominated by irresponsible transnational corporations and money lenders. Social democratic parties and governments should encourage nation states to introduce effective fiscal policies designed to restrict the present unregulated power of the transnationals.

Alternative Investment Mechanisms

The membership of the democratic socialist movement should promote alternative investment mechanisms. Organizations such as churches, credit unions, trade unions and co-operatives should be encouraged to invest a portion of their portfolios through mechanisms which contribute to the development of poor countries. Social democratic policy should encourage aid to governments attempting to meet the basic needs of their people through infrastructural projects such as those in the area of transportation, health or education.

Public Education

A key to gaining the widespread support needed to implement social democratic strategies is public education. Concomitantly, a new information order in which international media are not dominated by multinational corporations and where information links between north and south are encouraged is an important component of successful public education in developed countries.

THE ISSUE
Domestic Economies and the World

DISCUSSION

The fundamental questions which must be addressed and answered are common to all nation states. What determines:

where capital goes

what capital costs

the value of labour

the conditions attached to capital's use

the direction of domestic economic development

the beneficiaries of the free market flow of food and energy

?

There are no effective international public regulatory agencies to control the marketing of capital, food, energy and labour. Power and profit motivates the multinationals and transnationals which control the movement and use of these commodities. Consequently, the relationship between nations is largely exploitative. A co-operative, non-exploitative relationship between nations is a necessary corollary of inter-reliant nations whose people are in control of their own destinies. IMF and World Bank loans should reflect a co-operative approach to capital use and should recognize a nation's right to set its own economic development objectives.

We have forfeited public regulatory authority to the market, which distorts access to resources basic to human survival. We need international standards of judgment to value the basic resources of food, capital, labour and energy. We need a third party to regulate the relationship between multinationals and client nations. In light of Canada's relationship to the international economy and to existing international agencies, social democrats must press for a change in Canada's role. Social democrats should participate in the development of agencies which facilitate international co-operation to articulate economic and employment policy and to regulate access to, and distribution of, food, energy, labour and capital.

RECOMMENDATIONS

Transnational Fiscal Policy
Social democratic parties should push for the establishment of a Debtors' Fund, capitalized through subscription and borrowing from capital markets. The criteria for loans to developing countries should include improved human rights legislation, health and safety standards for workers, etc. Debts should be bought at discounted value from private banks when nations face default. Nations which default on current debts should be bailed out, even if the loan was for an undesirable purpose such as defence spending. However, nations will be warned that in the future they will be on their own when they borrow money for these purposes.

An international agency with authority over currency values and movement, and an international currency trading unit backed by a conglomeration of currencies should be established.

Domestic Banks
National policy should exert regulatory authority to control where, and for what purposes, major banks loan money. Such regulations could include higher reserve requirements for international, as opposed to national, loans. Banks should be forced to disclose more information about loans (for example, loans to whom, for what use, at what interest rates, under which special conditions). There should be riders on international loans from Canadian banks to guarantee that money is not loaned for defence spending or to nations with records of human rights abuse, but rather to those who require it to meet their basic needs strategy.

International Regulation of Food
New international agencies should be established to regulate the distribution, bartering and marketing of food. As well, new programs under existing United Nations agencies are needed to regulate trade in food and to ensure that imports are not made at the expense of indigenous agri-industry. Such agencies would regulate distribution, set quotas and regulate prices through negotiations to ensure that the needs of participating nations are met. An international land use inventory should be compiled. The United Nations Declaration of Human and Economic Rights should be updated. Social democrats should press for renewal of international commodity agreements to encourage mutually beneficial trading in food.

Energy
Canada, through international agencies and agreements, should strive for a more equitable sharing of global resources and the adoption of effective conservation policies. A world inventory of energy resources and potential should be developed. Developing nations should be encouraged to conduct research on alternative energy sources (for example,

geo-thermal, solar, wind). Savings from energy conservation in northern economies should be devoted, in part, to research into alternative energy sources and technology transfer programs. As part of our commitment to co-operative interreliance, Canada should offer helpful and benign technical information and expertise to developing nations.

Surplus energy resources should be transferred to energy deprived nations. Canada should consider mutually beneficial multilateral brokerage agreements with nations which want to pool or trade energy resources and develop mutually beneficial state-to-state energy trade. Export controls could be used to discourage Canadian companies from dumping energy resources, such as coal, on world markets in contravention of international agreements.

Canada should develop a code of ethics for transnational energy companies, especially petroleum multinationals. Petro-Canada should be responsive to the national interest of countries with which it enters into development and exploration agreements. Companies seeking exploration and development rights in developing countries should be required to transfer technology in return for these rights.

International Regulation of Labour
As a condition of most-favoured trading status, developing nations should be required to adopt International Labour Organizations Fair Labour Standards and the United Nations Charter of Human Rights. These international standards should be monitored and transgressions should result in the imposition of sanctions. Higher tariffs and other barriers could be used to penalize countries with poor labour standards. Labour standards should be treated as human rights. Canadian unions, through the Canadian Labour Congress, should be encouraged to assist trade unions in developing nations which adopt ILO standards and encourage international trade unionism to eliminate cheap labour pools. Export Processing Zones, based on poor labour standards, must be discouraged. An agreement like the Helsinki Accord should be promoted for the western hemisphere.

AUTHORS' BIOGRAPHICAL NOTES

Gregory Baum
Professor of Theology and Religious Studies, St. Michael's College. Editor, *The Ecumenist*, author of numerous books including *Catholics and Canadian Socialism.*

Margaret Lowe Benston
Computing Science and Women's Studies, Simon Fraser University. Author of a textbook on quantitative analysis and numerous articles on the impacts of science and technology on women.

Samuel Bowles
Professor of Economics, University of Massachusetts. Author of numerous books and articles on economics, education, class structure in the United States and contemporary economic issues. Served in 1969 as a consultant to the Ministries of Sugar, Education and Planning in Cuba.

Michael Cassidy
Former leader of the New Democratic Party in Ontario. Currently, MP for Ottawa Centre, NDP critic for Science and Technology, Treasury Board and the National Capital Commission. Alderman, City of Ottawa, 1969-72. Ottawa bureau chief, Financial Times of Canada, 1966-70.

Joop den Uyl
Alderman, Amsterdam 1962-65. Government of the Netherlands: Ministry of Economic Affairs 1943-45, Member Second Chamber, States General 1956-63, Minister, Economic Affairs 1965-66. Prime Minister and Minister of General Affairs 1973-77. Vice Prime Minister 1981-82, currently Chairman, Parliamentary Party.

John Fryer
M.A. Labour Economics (Pittsburgh). President, National Union of Provincial Government Employees. Vice President, Canadian Labour Congress. Member of the Labour Relations Board of British Columbia. Adjunct Associate Professor, University of Victoria.

Patricia McDermott
Ph.D. Sociology (Toronto), LL.B. (Osgoode Hall). Formerly taught at York University, the University of Toronto and the Labour College of Canada. Author of numerous publications on the effects of microtechnology and its use in corporate strategies.

George McRobie
B.Sc. Economics (London School of Economics). Chairman of the Board, Intermediate Technology Development Group Ltd. Author of *Small is Possible.* At various times, consultant to the Govern-

ments of Tanzania, Kenya, Ghana, India, Tasmania and Zimbabwe. Fellow of the Royal Society of Arts.

Clay Perry
B.A. Philosophy. Legislative Director, Western Regional Council, International Woodworkers of America. Formerly Executive Assistant, Minister of Health (B.C.), Special Assistant to the Minister of Labour and member of the Public Service Commission. Founding Member, Pacific Group for Policy Alternatives.

David Plotke
M.A. Sociology (California). Instructor in Sociology, University of California. Editor, *Socialist Review* (1976-81). Author of numerous publications on current sociological developments and applications of Marxist theory.

David Schreck
Ph.D. Economics (University of B.C.). Secretary, Pacific Group for Policy Alternatives. General Manager, CU&C Health Services Society.

Evan Simpson
Professor, McMaster University. Author of various publications on ethics, current philosophical issues and civil rights. Member of the Board of Directors of the Canadian Civil Liberties Association.

Lee Soderstrom
Professor of Economics, McGill University. Author of *The Canadian Health System* and numerous publications on health care delivery systems. Extensively involved in the public debate on extra billing.

Howard M. Wachtel
Ph.D. Economics (Michigan). Chairman, Department of Economics, The American University. Author of numerous publications including *Workers' Management and Workers' Wages in Yugoslavia* and *The New Gnomes: Multinational Banks in the Third World*.

Peter Warrian
Ph.D. History (Waterloo). Executive Assistant to the President, Ontario Public Service Employees Union. Formerly instructed at Conestoga Community College, University of Western Ontario, Niagara College and at many labour schools. Author of numerous publications on labour history, arbitration, issues in industrial relations and current economic developments.

CONFERENCE PARTICIPANTS
AND CO-AUTHORS

Terry Anderson • Cliff Andstein • Roy Bailey • Paul Barnett
Dave Barrett • Marc Belanger • Ruben Bellan
Margaret Benston • Erin Berger • Elaine Bernard
C.C. Bigelow • Sam Bowles • John Brewin
Douglas Broome • Rosemary Brown • Maurice Byblow
Gerry Caplan • Tony Charles • Helen Casher
Michael Cassidy • Darwin Charlton • Dr. Kes Chetty
Don Ching • Robert Clarke • Dennis Cocke
Yvonne Cocke • Judy Coffin • Rick Coleman
Joel Connelly • Joe Corsbie • Margaret Corsbie
Eileen Dailly • Johanna den Hertog • W. J. Dennison
Joop den Uyl • Enrique de Torres Lezema • Sharon DiGeso
Ginette Dussault • Marc Eliesen • Brian Emery
B. G. (Gene) Errington • Dr. John Foster • Anne Fraser
John Fryer • Colin Gabelmann, • Naomi Leigh Gadbois
John Gates • Robin Geary • Maurice Gibbons • Bill Goodacre
Rev. Art Griffen • Tom Gunton • Donald Gutstein
Anita Hagen • John Hagen • Leif Hansen • Michael Harcourt
John Harney • Rod Haynes • Carolyn Hilbert
Stephen Hilbert • Hector Hortie • Susan Irwin
Andrew Jackson • Pauline Jewett • Nel Joostema
Olga Kempo • Pat Kerwin • Lyle Kristiansen
Joy Langan • Stan Lanyon • Gary Lauk
Lorna Leader • David Levi • Norman Levi
Michael Lewis • Evan Lloyd • Dale Lovick • Clive Lytle
Douglas McArthur • John McCallum • Patricia McDermott
Alex Macdonald • Val Macdonald • Grace MacInnis
John McInnis • Brad McKenzie • Jim McKenzie • Joy McPhail
Mary Ellen McQuay • Sharon McRae • George McRobie
Michael Manley-Casimir • Kim Manning • Pat Marchak
Jacquie Maund • John Mika • Allen Mills
Margaret Mitchell • Terry Morley • Jim Morrison
Donna Mottershead • George Natsikas • Joyce Nash
Lorne Nicolson • Jerry Ochitwa • Don Olds
Corliss Olson • James Patterson • Raymond Payne
Patricia Portsmouth • Clay Perry • Dr. Tom Perry
David Plotke • Lise Poulin-Simon • Dick Proctor
George Reamsbottom • John Richards • Nelson Riis
Dennis Robideau • Svend Robinson • Roy Romanow
Mark Rose • Dr. Douglas Ross • Tim Roxburgh
Dr. Jim Russell • Susan Sanderson • Russ St. Eloi

Bob Schlosser • David Schreck • Vic Schroeder
Gerry Scott • Cliff Scotton • Robin Sears • Lloyd Shaw
Evan Simpson • Shane Simpson • Alasdair Sinclair
Lister Sinclair • Robert Skelly • Joan Smallwood
Hon. Muriel Smith • Frank Snowsell • Lee Soderstrom
Nicki Strong-Boag • David Stupich • Ron Taylor
Hilda Thomas • Sharon Vance • David Vickers
Howard Wachtel • Barbara Wallace • Nancy Walsh
John Warnock • Peter Warrian • Sophie Weremchuk
Ted Westlin • Alan Whitehorn • Joyce Whitman
Bob Williams • Gloria Williams • Donna Wilson
Harold Winch • Jessie Winch • Arlene Wortsman

INDEX

259

ORDER FORM

The editorial focus of this volume has been the papers prepared for the conference, and the group discussions. Many of the papers have been severely edited for length. Some, because they were not formally presented to discussion groups, have not been included in the text. Available from the Boag Foundation are the papers not included in the text and unedited papers which appear in abridged form (those which suffered only minor revisions are not included in this offer).

To order papers, please send an appropriate contribution to cover postage and handling to:

The Boag Foundation
576 Keith Road
West Vancouver, B.C.
Canada V7T 1L7

1. Baum, Gregory, "A Commentary of Laborem Exercens: Pope John Paul II's Socialism"
2. Benston, Margaret Lowe, "A New Technology But the Same Old Story"
3. Bowles, Samuel, "Wage-Led Growth: How to Break the Rules and Enjoy a Free Lunch"
4. Cassidy, Michael, "A Socialist Response to Technological Change"
5. McDermott, Patricia, "The Conscious Spirit of Resistance"
6. McRobie, George, "Technologies for Rich Countries"
7. Perry, Clay, "Democratic Socialism in a Hostile World"
8. Plotke, David, "The Future of Social Policy: A Response to the Conservative Critique of the Welfare State"
9. Simpson, Evan, "Prospects for a Moral Economy"
10. Soderstrom, Lee, "Government Stewardship of Health Services: Is It Necessary?"
11. Wachtel, Howard M., "Transnational Economy and Social Democracy"
12. Warrian, Peter, "Trade Unions and the New International Division of Labour"

Name _____

Address _____

_____ Code _____

Paper number _____ Author _____

Postage and handling enclosed _____

BOOKS OF INTEREST

From The Boag Foundation

THE LONG WINDING ROAD
Canadian Labour in Politics by Morden Lazarus — 2.50
PERTINENT PORTRAITS
C.C.F. 1934 by Barry Mather (illustrations by Fraser Wilson) — 2.00
SOMEWHERE — A PERFECT PLACE by Arthur J. Turner — 3.50

From New Star Books

AMERICA, THE LAST DOMINO
U.S. Foreign Policy in Central America under Reagan
by Stan Persky — 4.95
FAITH, HOPE, NO CHARITY
An Inside Look at the Born-Again Movement in Canada
and the United States by Judith Haiven — 7.95
LET US RISE!
A History of the Manitoba Labour Movement
by Doug Smith — 13.95
MY DEAR LEGS
Letters to a Young Social Democrat by Alex Macdonald — 7.95
THE NEW REALITY
The Politics of Restraint in B.C. by Warren Magnusson et al — 4.95
PARLIAMENT VS. PEOPLE
An Essay on Democracy and Canadian Political Culture
by Philip Resnick — 6.95
THE REAL PUSHERS
A Critical Analysis of the Canadian Drug Industry
by Joel Lexchin — 8.95

All titles are available from New Star Books, 2504 York Avenue, Vancouver, B.C., Canada V6K 1E3. Please make cheques payable to New Star Books. For shipping and handling, add $1 for the first book, 50¢ for each additional. New Star catalogues are available on request.